WAKE UP TO WHAT MATTERS

WAKE
UP TO
WHAT
MATTERS

A Guide to
Tibetan Buddhism
for the Next Generation

AVIKRITA VAJRA SAKYA

SHAMBHALA
BOULDER 2019

SHAMBHALA PUBLICATIONS, INC.
4720 Walnut Street
Boulder, Colorado 80301
www.shambhala.com

9 8 7 6 5 4 3 2 1

First Edition
Printed in the United States of America

♾ This edition is printed on acid-free paper that meets
the American National Standards Institute Z39.48 Standard.
♻ This book is printed on 30% postconsumer recycled paper.
For more information please visit www.shambhala.com.

Shambhala Publications is distributed worldwide by
Penguin Random House, Inc., and its subsidiaries.

Designed by Liz Quan

LIBRARY OF CONGRESS CATALOGING-IN-PUBLICATION DATA
Names: Avikrita Vajra Sakya, Rinpoche, 1993- author.
Title: Wake up to what matters: a guide to Tibetan Buddhism for the
next generation/Avikrita Vajra Sakya.
Description: First edition. | Boulder, Colorado: Shambhala, 2019.
Identifiers: LCCN 2018050874 |
ISBN 9781611806601 (pbk.: alk. paper)
Subjects: LCSH: Dharma (Buddhism) | Buddhism—China—
Tibet Autonomous Region—Doctrines. | Buddhism—21st century.
Classification: LCC BQ4190.A95 2019 | DDC 294.3/923—dc23
LC record available at https://lccn.loc.gov/2018050874

CONTENTS

THE DALAI LAMA

Wake Up to What Matters, a book by Khondung Avikrita Vajra Sakya Rinpoche of the Sakya Phuntsog family, elucidates many philosophical ideas and practices of Buddhism. At a time when interest in Buddhist philosophy is increasing throughout the world, this book is an additional resource, making the knowledge accessible in a contemporary, readable manner.

Rinpoche has received education in classical Buddhism as well as knowledge and explains the general structure of Buddhism and how to apply it in our daily lives. I hope readers will find this book helpful.

June 6, 2019

FOREWORD

Abhaya Vajra Sakya

Before I became a monk, I had short dark hair and round spectacles, and due to my brother's appearance, some people used to jokingly refer to us as Tibetan Superman and Harry Potter. Now I have a shaved head and square glasses, so I don't get called Harry Potter anymore, but my brother is still Superman, and not just because of his looks. Here's why.

About his name. Being a Tibetan Buddhist leader, he's formally known as Khöndung Avikrita Vajra Rinpoche. The title *Khöndung* means "son of the Khön family," an important spiritual lineage from Tibet. Avikrita Vajra is his actual name. It's Sanskrit rather than Tibetan because that's the original language of Mahayana Buddhism, which we follow, and it means something like "Unchanging Diamond Thunderbolt." *Rinpoche* (a title for respected Tibetan lamas) is a title most people use to address him, as it is both affectionate and respectful; it means "precious jewel." On top of that, his Tibetan Dharma name is Ngawang Kunga Thegchog Gyurme Dorje Tashi Dragpai Gyaltsen Pal Zangpo (a lot of names, huh?), but generally we just call him Avi Rinpoche.

Avi Rinpoche was born in Seattle, Washington, in 1993. Although he is Tibetan, he was born there because our family settled there in 1960, having had to flee Tibet due to the Chinese occupation. They were able to relocate thanks to a Rockefeller Foundation sponsorship at the invitation of the Tibetan Studies Program at the University of Washington. When our father, who was the first Tibetan born in America, grew up, he spent some time in Taiwan to learn Mandarin, and there he met a fellow Tibetan who was the younger daughter of a student of our grandfather. They fell in love, tied the knot, and went back to Seattle together to start a family of their own.

The first four years of Avi Rinpoche's life were spent in America, until our parents decided to bring him to India so he could undergo the traditional training required to be a fully qualified spiritual leader. Eventually, he moved to the Sakya Center in Dehradun. While studying the basics of Tibetan Buddhism, Avi Rinpoche also received many precious teachings and initiations from His Holiness Jigdal Dagchen Sakya, His Holiness the Sakya Trichen, and many other respected masters of the tradition.

Recognizing the need for a base for Avi Rinpoche to deepen his training, His Holiness Jigdal Dagchen Sakya established the Sakya Heritage Society for the family's spiritual tradition in New Delhi. As soon as it opened in 2005, Avi Rinpoche moved there with his tutors and some fellow students. For the hot Indian summers, he would move to Darjeeling, where he studied the Vajrakila tantric rituals, a sacred practice of the Sakya tradition that is performed by Tibetan masters annually, as has been done continuously for many centuries.

After three years of rigorous study, he performed the Vajrakila ritual as chant master at the Sakya Center perfectly, then as ritual leader for the same ceremony in Ghoom Monastery in Darjeeling, to which our grandmother Dagmo Kusho said that it made her feel relieved that the future of the lineage was safe with him.

Of course, banging a drum and chanting were not the only things he learned over the years. At the age of thirteen, he undertook his first meditation retreat with the great meditation master Luding Khenchen Rinpoche. He later conducted another important retreat in Darjeeling, and upon its completion many people said that they saw auspicious signs. Before moving to college, he went into another meditation retreat to develop his intuitive wisdom in order to maximize his capacity for learning. Those retreats qualified Avi Rinpoche to lead certain rituals and teach advanced meditative practices.

In 2010, at the age of seventeen, to penetrate the deep philosophical tradition of the Sakya school, Avi Rinpoche enrolled at Dzongsar Institute in Himachal Pradesh. There he studied the classic treatises of Buddhist philosophy that came from the ancient Nalanda University of India, such as Nagarjuna's root treatise on the Middle Way, and later important Tibetan texts, such as Sakya Pandita's *Treasury of Valid Cognition and Reasoning*. Although that takes so much of his time, he still makes time to fulfill his personal pledge to attend the Vajrakila rituals each year and, during his winter break, travels to receive teachings from great masters such as His Holiness Jigdal Dagchen Sakya, and has now started to share his knowledge, teaching people across the globe with his blend of traditional wisdom and empathetic understanding of the modern world.

Although he has achieved so much in his training and activities as a young Buddhist teacher, that's not enough to know the real Tibetan Superman. After not seeing him for many years while I was growing up in Seattle, I came to see his qualities and how cool he really is, not just because he's my older brother but also because of how he is as a person and spiritual guide. He was actually my inspiration to move to India to train in a Buddhist monastery.

Back in 2013, when I wanted to do my first meditation retreat, Avi Rinpoche gave up his free time from college and came all the way down to Delhi from the Himalayan foothills to bestow the initiation I needed and to teach me how to do the retreat. This is just one example of how he is always so generous, patient, caring, and kind. Avi Rinpoche has a real passion for learning new things, having received an enormous amount of teachings, knowing four languages, and being always eager to ask questions. He never shows anger, never criticizes anyone, and always seems to look at the bright side of things. Of course he is passionate about Buddhism, but he is also passionate about teaching environmental protection, stopping discrimination and bullying, and promoting equality. He always thinks about others' happiness rather than his own. He is also very accommodating, easy to relate to, and always willing to listen to the people who come seeking his advice and blessings.

This highlights just a few of his great qualities, as it's hard to explain all of them and would use a lot of paper! You'll have to meet this guy to know how he really is. He's a Buddhist teacher like no other, which is why I'm sure you'll find this book refreshing and mind-opening. Just as the book's author has helped and guided me and many others in our lives, I hope this book will similarly bring immense benefit to you too.

INTRODUCTION

Soon after I started giving Dharma teachings in the West, English-speaking friends who heard these talks began to make requests for the teachings to be made available in print. I have to admit, when I was approached on the subject, I flatly declined, because I feel that I have nothing original to say. I'm really just passing on what I have learned from my own teachers. In fact, in most of my talks I'm really talking to myself more than anyone else. However, when these requests reached the ear of my late grandfather, His Holiness Jigdal Dagchen Sakya, and he expressed the wish for a book to be made, I couldn't say no.

My grandfather remains my hero and inspiration. He was a highly respected and renowned Buddhist teacher in Tibet who came to the United States in 1960, working tirelessly to preserve Buddhist teachings and make them available to people who wished to learn all over the world. I was born in the United States and spent my earliest years with him and my family before moving to India in order to undergo traditional training to be a lama (Tibetan Buddhist teacher) in the monasteries of our tradition. I was fortunate enough that I could continue to see my grandfather and learn from him whenever he visited India or other parts of Asia, and I also made a few visits to the United States to see him as much as possible. During those precious times, he explained many special aspects of Tibetan Buddhist teachings, and of our Sakya tradition in particular, that he wished for me to learn well and even contribute in reviving in the future. There was so much I learned from him that when the time came shortly before he passed away, I asked with a sense of urgency what was the most important goal he wanted me to focus on. I had my notebook out, ready to write down the names of some rituals he perhaps wanted done in the monasteries or rare Buddhist yogic practices he would want me to teach in the future as he had done before. But he didn't go into any of that. He simply said, "Connecting with people; bringing people together in compassion." With that inspiration and determination, I hope this book can be a small start to the work I've set my heart on.

The reflections in this book are edited transcripts from various teachings, talks, and words of advice that I was asked to give in America, England, Hong Kong, and other parts of the world between 2013 and 2016. In most cases, the original talks I gave were more reflective than academic. In our traditional training in Tibetan Buddhism, we would normally want a published book to use quite a scholarly framework. However, as was pointed out to me when I first shied away from the idea of publishing my talks, a less formal style may prove to be a good thing in that it can perhaps make the teachings as comprehensible as possible for newcomers to Buddhist ideas who may be interested in this book.

So before the book begins, I wish to express my appreciation to Venerable Ngawang Khyentse who took the full responsibility of transcribing and editing all my talks for the book, as well as Dr. Nick Swann and Casey Kemp for all their hours of hard work to prepare the text for publication.

WAKE UP TO WHAT MATTERS

1

Buddhism for the Next Generation

Let's take a look at the Dharma for... how can I put this? Well, for those of us who aren't old-timers! Actually, the Dharma is for everyone: young and old, Easterner and Westerner, Northerner and Southerner, big and small, able-bodied and differently abled-bodied, male and female, and any other gender identity, straight, gay, bi, black, white, and any other color in the rainbow as far as I'm concerned. We're all the same. We're all members of the one human family, all looking to find happiness, to find meaning in our lives, to find freedom from stress, confusion, and pain. But, understanding how we all have our own unique DNA, our own special needs, desires, qualities, habits, and so on, the Buddha made sure to bestow a vast range of teachings and practices so that we could each relate to the Dharma in a way that really resonates for us. That's what the Dharma is for, actually: whatever it takes to awaken the buddha within all of us.

We've got this word *Buddhism* in English; people generally call it a religion. When people think of Buddhism, a lot of the time they think of shaven heads and robes, cross-legged dudes staring at their navels for hours on end, chanting, and all that. But whatever—that's just like the window dressing of the store. What's actually inside the store is not a religion just to be believed in—we have to go in and make use of what's on offer inside. What we call the Dharma is like a whole way of life. In essence, it's the way of wisdom and compassion.

The Verbalized Dharma and the Realized Dharma

There's no exact word to translate *Dharma* into English, but generally speaking, it means two things: there's the verbalized Dharma and there's the realized Dharma.

The verbalized Dharma means the teachings that the Buddha gave: one part is mostly about the best way of living in the world, the moral way that allows us to live without heavy, sticky feelings of guilt, without creating stress for ourselves or others; one part is mostly about how to train the mind, how to purify the disturbing emotions such as anger, jealousy, and so on that aren't part of our true nature but are like dark clouds that temporarily hide the sun of our mind's true nature underneath—that's what meditation is about; and one is about the nature of reality, the teachings that we study, contemplate, and meditate on to gain a deep understanding of truth.

The truth is what sets us free. When we see the truth directly—not just a hunch, or through a blind faith, or even through being smart in the regular sense, but through awakened wisdom, a knowing that is beyond all stains or blocks—then we're home; we awaken the buddha within us; we have the realized Dharma. The Dharma means the Buddha's dispensation of teachings and practices, and the truth of the way things really are, which the Buddha pointed out, the seeing of which liberates us from all suffering.

Looking into the deeper sense of what the Dharma is for us is really important, because we can say "I'm a Buddhist," or "I'm from a Buddhist family," or "I'm interested in Buddhism," and we can wear a *mala* around our wrists and learn how to ring bells and rattle the hand drums, and we can even receive special tantric initiations and all of that—but if we don't have the deeper sense of what the Dharma is for, then . . . big deal! It wouldn't be much different from wearing a uniform for some weekend club that we go to, learning all the ropes, going along to please our parents, or because—well, it beats watching reruns of talk shows all afternoon.

The point is that discovering the precious jewel of Dharma is better than winning the lottery, better than anything else we could ever wish for. It doesn't just fulfill our own hopes and dreams; it benefits all sentient beings. So what a waste if we don't cash in that magic lottery ticket.

Now, the thing is—when I was a young teen, I sometimes thought, "Whoa, there's so much I have to learn. There are all these weird words and long prayers and complicated texts I have to remember. There are all these elaborate rituals I need to learn. There are all these rules I have to get right. I have to get my meditation on track. . . . Being a Buddhist looks like pretty hard work, doesn't it?" But then I remembered something the Buddha said: the woodlands are so huge, but we only need a handful of leaves to know the entire forest. He also said that we don't need to train in a huge number of things; we can achieve our goals by focusing on one thing: compassion. This I found so encouraging.

If we go in deeply, we can explore Buddhist ethics, Buddhist psychology, Buddhist science. We can say it that way. But if we really want to feel the benefits of the Dharma in our lives, and if we really want it to enable us to create a better world for the sake of those we share the world with, then we can't relate to the Dharma as something on paper or in our brains separate from what happens in our hearts. In other words, the Dharma is something very practical—it's never a theory separate from practice.

This emphasis on the practicality of Dharma is so important for us because we can't sit around waiting for the Buddha to float down on a magic lotus to wash away our problems and make us see the light by laying his hands on our heads. The Buddha isn't our god. He came into the world to point to the truth, to point out the greatest potential that we as humans could evolve into, but it's up to us to put what he taught into practice.

A Refuge

When we're in a really bad storm, we run for somewhere we know will be safe to escape the fears and perils of the tempest, don't we? In a similar way, when we recognize the crazy, violent storm that we're in the middle of with afflictive emotions and confusions, we go for refuge to the Buddha as the one who can show us a safe passage out of this danger. Going for refuge means this is an ongoing process—a process until we become our own refuge. That's our goal. So the Buddha is the one who shows us the path; the Dharma is the path itself; and the Sangha means the companionship of bodhisattvas (compassionate beings on the different levels of awakening), who help us walk the path to truth and freedom. Together, they make up what we refer to as the three jewels of refuge, and by taking refuge in them from our hearts, we can call ourselves official Buddhists, walkers of the way of wisdom and compassion that leads to liberation and enlightenment.

The Wings of Wisdom and Compassion

For us so-called Buddhists, I think two things have to go together for us to keep it real, like two wings for takeoff: wing number one is compassion, and wing number two is wisdom. When we've got both, then—liftoff!

To develop wisdom, first of all, of course we have to learn. For that, we've got the texts—books on mind training (*lojong*), philosophy, and so on. But we might feel that it's hard to take in a lot of reading with all our homework assignments and work and so on. So even if we can't read a lot, at least we can look at some of the essential teachings, such as the Buddha's verses in the *Dhammapada*, or Shantideva's *Entering the Bodhisattva's Way of Life*, or *The Thirty-*

Seven Practices of a Bodhisattva by Gyalse Thogme, and books like that. Those are texts I found really helpful to look at on my own before I even started studying formally. Since they're written in verse—mostly four-line stanzas—if we read just one verse a day, then even if we're really busy, our hearts will open and our minds will grow, bit by bit. And then since we can't develop deep wisdom just from reading, we also need to hear, to listen—so going to the teachings of great masters, of learned and experienced nuns and monks and so forth, will really help enrich our minds.

But even if we look at sacred verses or listen to amazing teachings, it's hard to really mature our minds if our emotions are all over the place. This isn't only when we're a complete wreck with rage or desire; it can be when we're just zoning out a lot, distracted, uptight, stressed; when we've lost perspective and clarity because those clouds of confusion and tension have drifted onto our horizon again. What can really help us come down from all that *grrrrr!* into a calm, grounded state of being is mindfulness and vigilance.

Mindfulness is like a cool, awesome energy that gives continuity and stability to our sense of calm, confidence, and clarity. Vigilance is like its twin, the aspect of our awareness that keeps disturbing emotions at bay.

One of the main ways we practice mindfulness and vigilance is to follow the calm flow of breathing in and out, and up and down through our bodies. We're so used to being stuck up in our heads, dissociated from what we're really experiencing, what we're really feeling in the here and now. So this gives us back our ground. When we first try it, it's not all sunshine and cheerful chirping birds. Often, we'll notice some uncomfortable feelings inside—cold and numb in the lower back, or highly charged and blocked in the solar plexus, or tight and hard in the neck and shoulders. But with greater awareness, we're *with* those feelings instead of being stuck *in* them. This is the Buddha's gift to us: to find freedom instead of being a slave to afflictive emotions.

When we're *with* the difficult bits, we've straightaway got the insight that yes, it hurts, but they're not permanent; they're creases in the fabric that we can iron out. We can experience the ending of all that. The calm mind flows up and down with the breathing like it's riding the tides of the breath. It's like an inner-body massage. When we do this, it's actually an act of kindness to ourselves; it's love and compassion that starts *here*. Then, as we really experience our whole body and mind feeling more soft, smooth, and open, we can extend that warmth, that light, that love out to others. Even the people who have crossed the line with us and caused us or our loved ones pain— they have only acted out because of the afflictions such as jealousy and fear that they've become stuck in, so we can even spread that healing light to them. We don't have to cross our legs and burn incense sticks to do this, though of course it helps to do it in a more concentrated way. The most important thing is to have self-confidence, to trust in our own buddha within.

If we remember to check in every day with what's happening on Planet You with full, open awareness, even if it's just a few minutes between our everyday activities, we'll really notice positive changes. Otherwise, we're just left with the story lines playing out on our inner movie screens: "He said, she said; then I said and—it's not fair. What if I...? If only I could.... Why's he doing it that way? I mean, what's it all about, man? *Bla, bla, bla-dee bla-dee bla....*" Yeah, our own personal soap opera goes on and on and on. Awakening calm and insight means we can remember where the off switch is. And even when all that nonsense just won't shut up, we've got a tool to not get caught up and suffer over it all, to stay grounded, to not be overwhelmed.

This general theme is what I think is most important as a foundation for however we want to use and develop Dharma. Maybe we want to explore deeper teachings, to inquire about the nature of reality, but it won't be integrated, and it won't go beyond concepts if we haven't opened the door of empathetic awareness. And maybe we want to learn how to do some of these beautiful rituals and prayers and so on, but it could just be a lot of mumbo-jumbo if we haven't set our hearts in the right direction first. Even if we want to meditate, it will be a struggle to process all that's going on in the mind when we sit on the cushion if we don't have that mindfulness in our everyday life—the momentum and effects of unprocessed feelings will be too strong.

All We've Got to Do Is Practice

Life isn't easy sometimes, right? But if we put our trust in the foundations for wisdom and compassion like this, then the potential for positive change in our lives is really awesome. We can calm the waves on the ocean of mind and discover really beautiful things underneath. All we've got to do is practice.

Now when I say practice, it's not all about what goes on in our inner world. According to the Dharma, our inner world and our outer world are interdependent, so if we're awakening love and compassion and wisdom, it has to express itself. We've got to dream out loud. Some people—well, I'll be honest here, some of the old-fashioned monks—might get a bit fed up with me always going on about the environment and animal welfare, and my stuff about stopping bullying, but hopefully these ideas about how we've got to help our world will resonate with you, because as His Holiness the Dalai Lama always says, the future of the world is in our generation's hands. We're the generation that has to act—and act now—to create changes inside and out. I'm really hopeful that with the resource of Dharma that we have, our dreams will become reality.

2

Discovering the Riches of Buddhism

Let's begin by reflecting—with joy—on how fortunate we are to have discovered the jewel of Dharma that is Buddhism. In this sense, we're all very fortunate to possess such a precious jewel, and what a shame it would be if we wasted it. We should instead put it to good use.

It's not just when our lives are comfortable and easygoing that we remember and practice the Dharma; it is especially important when we consider the many problems that come and go in our world and also when we are in the midst of difficulties ourselves that we really invest in this jewel of the Buddha's dispensation.

What It Means to Be Fortunate

First, I should explain how we use terms such as *riches* and *being fortunate*. After studying some sociology, I saw that modern schools of thought usually consider economic factors to be the dominant condition that affects our lives the most. In ordinary terms, most people tend to think that being fortunate means having lots of money, property, commodities, and so on—these are the things that are usually considered riches. That is materialism.

This is not the case in Mahayana Buddhism, the altruistic system of Buddhism for attaining full awakening to benefit all sentient beings. Some people might think that because the Buddha gave up all material possessions and became a very simple wandering monk, all Buddhists must idealize poverty, but that is definitely not the case. In fact, it is taught that of the qualities of a fortunate life that help us practice Buddhism, such as a good family, a healthy body, a smart brain, and so on, one is the quality of wealth—at least having enough material resources to practice Buddhism. Right from the very beginning of Shakyamuni Buddha's own teaching activity, he pointed out the limiting extremes of views and practices that were either overly materialistic on the one hand or self-punishing on the other. He advocated what is known as the middle way.

The Middle Way

Now, the middle way is not just a boring compromise between worldly life and religious life that the Buddha invented. He first explained what he had discovered through his enlightenment (known in Sanskrit as *bodhi*, or "awakening") in terms of the eightfold path and then elaborated on this in the Mahayana teachings with the five progressive paths of the bodhisattvas. In essence, he gave innumerable teachings on the best kind of moral conduct, meditation, and understanding that we need to develop for our temporal and ultimate happiness.

Among those teachings, he said, for example that poverty would lead to ethical standards declining in our communities, such as people stealing to get what they need, and counseled rulers and citizens with very skillful means to combat poverty.

As important as that is, still, everything is impermanent, and when we reach the end of our lives, how many dollars, how many businesses, how many houses can we take with us to the next life? None. So while the Buddha pointed to our innate interconnectedness—or what he called dependent origination—of factors that determine our welfare, and so recognized the part that material matters have to play in social stability and personal well-being, the Buddha emphasized the spiritual riches that bring benefit not just to this life but to all our future lives too.

That's why, when he became the Buddha, he didn't give up being a monk and go back to living in a royal palace. You know, he wouldn't have said, "Hey, now can I swap my robes and bowl for an Armani suit and an iPod?" No, he continued to walk through India as a simple monk to share these teachings so that as many people as possible could discover the very same spiritual riches that he had discovered, so that whether monk, nun, or lay-practitioner, they could become awakened heroes, bodhisattvas, free from all suffering and able to continue and expand the Dharma that can free everyone from all suffering. He called such beings *aryans*, which is an ancient Indian term that means something like "noble," but the Buddha didn't mean it like an inherited nobility, rather, a nobility that is acquired from inner qualities.

So, what exactly are the riches of the aryans?

Faith

First, let's look at faith. Since I was very young, I was brought up around devout Buddhist people, but I didn't really know much about Buddhism. If there was a teaching or empowerment, I just went along to receive it without even knowing what the meaning or benefits were. It was just like a show to me, and I didn't really know what was going on. But as I grew up, my maternal grandfather told me many stories about the masters who I received the teachings from and how they became so learned and accomplished. After hearing all of these amazing biographies, I became so inspired and regretted all the time I had been distracted and not properly appreciated the great masters from whom I received teachings and so on. Since then, I have seen my teachers very differently and have immense faith in all of them.

When we talk about faith in Buddhism, it's really important to emphasize that this does not mean *blind* faith—a belief in dogma that we subscribe to, whether it leads to virtue or not, because some higher power is supposed to have said so. Rich faith in Buddhism is a *reliable* faith—faith that, due to causes that we have looked at ourselves, is a trust and even a passion for something authentic that makes virtue arise in our minds.

And what is that special "something" that we have such conviction in? That is the Triple Gem: the Buddha who shows us the path; the verbalized and realized Dharma, which is the path; and the Sangha, especially the companionship of aryan bodhisattvas, who assist us on the path. In the tradition of Buddhism that is followed in Tibet (Vajrayana, the tantric school of Mahayana Buddhism), we also give paramount importance to the guru (spiritual master). Although we haven't had the fortune to meet the historical Buddha Shakyamuni in the flesh, we consider a kind and authentic teacher to be the embodiment of the Triple Gem because they grant empowerments and teachings that enable us to participate in the higher tantric practices to realize our buddha nature in this lifetime.

We can go for refuge to the Triple Gem and the guru out of a kind of fear—quite understandably, we're scared to face the consequences of unvirtuous karma (our intentional actions) in this and future lives, so we go for refuge in order to escape the vicious cycle of a suffering existence.

Then, if we are to go for refuge more from faith, first we need to have trust or belief in the guru and Triple Gem. To have that trust means that we don't just make a hasty decision like, "Oh, yeah, I heard Richard Gere is a Buddhist and I enjoyed one of his movies, so I guess I'll be a Buddhist now," or because our parents tell us we should—that is, without real consideration of the teachings. We develop that trust and belief through our own skillful reflection. When we have that, then that trust becomes real enthusiasm.

Just to see or think of the guru and Triple Gem will instantly make us feel inspired and relieved and comforted, a little like when we think of someone we love. Then our faith will become a yearning. When we just think of the Buddha and his amazing qualities, then instantly we yearn to attain those qualities ourselves because we have informed faith in the Buddha. Then, when we have developed that trust, enthusiasm, and yearning, we can develop our faith into full confidence. Because we have investigated what Buddhism is about and feel conviction that our liberation and enlightenment is truly possible through the path, we feel an unshakable assurance.

As I mentioned, blind faith is totally insufficient, but so is a purely intellectual approach to Buddhism. For example, some modern scholars have written books on what they call Buddhist meditation or mindfulness but disparage belief in rebirth and want to create a totally secular and materialist or psychotherapeutic approach to Buddhism—but how is that even Buddhism? The kind of faith that is full confidence means it is inextricable from reason and logic, but not just the common kind relating only to sensory phenomena.

As we study in the Buddhist science of epistemology (*pramana* in Sanskrit), in order to perceive ordinary sensory phenomena, we only require consciousness through sense organs that are unimpaired and so on. With phenomena that are not so evident, we're not just consigned to either believe in them because the Buddha talked about them or not believe because we can't see them. With subtler phenomena, we require subtler states of consciousness, which can be achieved through developing deep calm-abiding meditation, and then what was not evident before becomes evident to our minds. Even very obscure phenomena such as other realms and previous lives are evident phenomena to realized meditators. And we can achieve and sustain a calm-abiding meditation only if we have faith.

With faith, we will be able to have real trust in the Buddha as well as firm confidence in our own potential—which will make our going for refuge very strong; with faith, we will be able to dispel the hindrances to calm-abiding meditation—which will then lead to special insight. And since the felt sense of faith is what will bring us out of being stuck in our heads and down into our hearts to really activate our practice of Buddhism, we can see why faith is one of the riches of Buddhism.

Charity

Next, let's look at charity.

As the third-century Indian Buddhist scholar Aryadeva said, "Just the word *giving* is always of interest to bodhisattvas." Why is that? Well, first of all, by giving, we overcome its opposite, which is being selfish. Whether or not someone has some ego-centered thoughts floating around in the brain, if they behave in a way that is mean and selfish, they become like a stink in the room that we all naturally drift away from.

Selfishness stems from attachment. The more obvious kinds of selfishness directly inhibit giving, which is stronger in those who just don't get what karma is about, who might think, "Why should I give the monastic community donations? That won't bring me or my family any benefits! I'd rather spend my money on the new iPhone." There are also more subtle forms of selfishness that taint our acts of charity with ulterior motives, like thinking, "I know—I'll give the monks a donation and then post photos of it on Twitter and Facebook so everyone will think I'm such a good Buddhist." For those who connect with Mahayana Buddhism and generate the aspiration to attain the stage of a buddha for the sake of all sentient beings, when they conjoin their pure generosity with wisdom, it is the very first of a bodhisattva's six transcendent perfections (*paramitas* in Sanskrit). These are the practical aspects of *bodhichitta*—the compassionate determination to attain full awakening for the benefit of all sentient beings and acting upon that aspiration.

Not only will charity lead to the ultimate welfare of oneself and all sentient beings, it will bring many temporal benefits, such as creating the causes and conditions for obtaining the necessities of life, prosperity, a good reputation, better rebirth, and so on.

Morality

Next, let's look at morality, or moral conduct, which is also the second of the transcendent perfections when conjoined with wisdom in Mahayana Buddhism.

Sometimes people mistakenly think of morality a bit negatively, like it's a bunch of out-of-date lists of boring religious rules. Or some think that the purification of our minds can be separated from how we live our lives, like a guy going on a meditation course one weekend, then cheating on his partner and drunkenly spreading malicious gossip at a bar the next weekend. Some think that it's just so many shoulds and shouldn'ts that they can't keep up with and leaves them feeling guilty a lot of the time. Some think that morality means doing what they're told by some higher power—a person or text—no matter what others or they themselves feel to be right. Personally, I can't relate to morality in any of those ways. Actually, I think morality is something cool.

The way the Buddha referred to morality—or in Sanskrit *shila*, which literally means "to cool down"—was to behave physically, verbally, and mentally in a way that cools down the mind from the heat of the afflictions that create a haze on reality. Buddhists relate to moral conduct as behaving in accord with natural law, attuning our conduct to the way things are just as we do with our minds. So in order to be a richness, our commitment to moral conduct must be something that we choose to adopt from a place of skillful consideration—consideration of the way our karma determines our own and others' welfare. In order to be able to determine a solid commitment to morality, we must analyze the causes and conditions for immorality, or what are known as degrading misdeeds, because they will degrade our lives with suffering and stress and degrade our future lives into the lower states too. When we really look at it, we will see that all the degrading misdeeds stem from attachment, aggression, and delusion. So our commitments to live by a moral code in tune with truth must be in tandem with working to overcome the latent force of mental defilements. This insight means that although, for example, we could do something deceitful to gain some short-term profit, in the long term that degrading misdeed will only lead to loss of fortune and even more suffering, so we reject that kind of nonvirtue and live by virtue, which brings us fortune both short term and long term.

Now, the true nature of our minds is pure, beyond the temporary defilements like anger and so on. As we work to actualize that reality, we can remedy those forces provisionally, like cultivating compassion to overcome that anger and thereby the aggressive words we might end up saying and the karmic consequences that would follow. The ultimate antidote, though, as Dharmakirti explained in his *Commentary on Epistemology*, is to be liberated by seeing voidness, the ultimate reality. The more we purify our minds and get closer to seeing truth, the more we will stop misdirecting our thinking and behaving in ways that we will come to regret.

Enriching morality, then, is a commitment to conduct that is physically, verbally, and mentally virtuous and to avoiding conduct that is unvirtuous; it is based on a rich understanding. On that basis, we adopt the vows of a lay practitioner, or the novice vows, or the vows of a monk or nun. Then we don't do stupid things due to peer pressure; we don't get involved in corruption or think we can postpone moral conduct for later in life or something silly like that, because we have insight into what that would lead to.

Then those of great spiritual capacity cultivate a morality that is even richer by performing deeds that will really benefit others through giving what is needed, materially and spiritually; friendly communication; living a useful life; and living in accord with what is really meaningful.

As it is a natural law that hurting others is bad, to refrain from hurting others is very powerful. If we make a personal commitment or vow before the guru and Triple Gem, that we will refrain from hurting others, then our personal morality aligns with natural morality and becomes even more powerful. So the power and merit of morality is very, very great.

Personal and Social Conscience

Now, in order to have that morality, to empower it and to sustain it, we can look at another two riches of the aryans, which kind of go together: personal conscience and social conscience.

A personal and social conscience is always a virtuous state of mind, a richness that humans can enjoy if they wish to make their lives really meaningful. It's not an anxious sense of feeling guilty all the time, which is a kind of darkness in the mind. It's also not just feeling embarrassed at something tacky we did in the past–that's nothing special.

For example, when I first went to stay at the Sakya Center, an important Buddhist monastery in India, I was still a small boy. Many monks were awaiting my arrival, very formally with offering-scarves, ceremonial music, and so on. When I got out of the car, I followed some senior teachers who led me up the stairs to my quarters above the temple. As I climbed the stairs of the temple, all the monks below watched me, and I could hear some laughing behind me. Because I was still very young and self-conscious about my new position as a future teacher of the tradition, I was like, "What are they laughing about? Did I do something wrong? Am I walking funny?" Suddenly, I could feel my tutor behind me pulling on something. I turned around and noticed he was trying to tie my lower robe, which had become loose at the back so everyone could see my Spiderman underpants! Fortunately I've outgrown them; I can dress myself and have more mindfulness, but my hair still stands on end with embarrassment when I remember that day.

What I really want to point to is a conscience, which means that we feel, we know, deep down, how our actions of body, speech, and mind affect ourselves and others karmically. In this way, a healthy sense of shame, honor, and propriety is instilled in our minds, which is a brightness in the heart. This empowers us to feel self-confidence and self-respect and to be relaxed and happy in the company of others. While it is common to see Tibetan Buddhist paintings of rather fierce-looking protector deities such as Mahakala, it is personal and social conscience that the Buddha said were the two brightest protectors of the world. If we don't have personal and social conscience, don't expect much help from Mahakala!

As the great Indian Buddhist adept Shantideva said in *Entering the Bodhisattva's Way of Life*, even very educated people who have faith and diligence will still commit degrading misdeeds if they lack introspection. So we're looking at a dynamic process here; we're cultivating an awareness that guides our whole way of life. We're taking responsibility for our own karma rather than asking the Buddha or some god to do it for us. And then we're living by the insight that the self-control that stems from shame is not something that prevents us from feeling free and having fun, but rather it is a liberating experience.

Again, this is in tune with the natural order, with reality. We don't feel ashamed of something that is not shameful. For example, hurting a fellow human being is naturally harmful. Anyone who does it should expect their conscience to be bruised. They will feel bad inside and others will not respect them. Natural law is not the same as the changeable norms and values of society. For example, at one time women had little or no power or freedom in many countries because of various policies and customs, but that has nothing to do with real morality. These days, in America women are our doctors, our teachers, our elected representatives, and isn't it wonderful? If others criticize a woman for trying to achieve an equal career to a man, they are not speaking from a moral viewpoint but just old-fashioned conditioning. If we have the richness of a strong social conscience, it will not stop us from realizing our dreams and achieving a more peaceful, prosperous, ecologically sound, and fair society for everyone.

Because we're all interconnected, we should encourage one another in wholesome pursuits, instill a sense of responsibility in one another, and discourage one another from involvement in harmful pursuits.

Without personal and social conscience, we cannot respect ourselves, let alone our mothers, our sisters, our teachers, and so on. So we must feel enthusiastic about developing a rich personal and social conscience: a sense of personal dignity, of shame at nonvirtue; since our lives are all interconnected, we must feel even a sense of dread at the effects of harmful acts on others. This will then protect and guide our own lives in virtue and also bring social stability and benefits for our communities and eventually the whole planet. With these riches, the power to change our own lives as well as the world we live in is right here in the palm of our hand.

Learning

The Buddha also spoke about the development of our understanding as a richness; that we as capable human beings can utilize our intelligence as such a richness that it will overcome the transient afflictive emotions that disturb the heart and purify what obscures our primordial wisdom.

Now, we can fill our brains with all sorts of clever facts and ideas, but that doesn't necessarily enrich our lives or our society. For instance, some really learned guys work hard to develop more and more destructive weapons that kill many sentient beings. That's not the kind of learning we're interested in. Also, someone might have a learning difficulty such as dyslexia but still have a deep understanding of and commitment to morality and meditation, so I would call that person very intelligent actually. If we have an open heart and an upright mind, then whatever we learn that we apply to the practice of Dharma will yield fruit.

In one popular Tibetan Buddhist prayer, this development of understanding is called "learning for liberating the mind stream." Whether listening carefully to the words of our teachers or studying texts, in Buddhism there is no real separation of theory and practice. Whether something is worth learning or not depends on whether it is then useful to contemplate and meditate on, and whether it will free our mind streams from defilements and help bring happiness to the world. Without the richness of learning, we are blind. We will lack the foundation for thorough investigation to know what is worth pursuing and what is not, and then our actions will be ineffectual. Learning is the starting point for removing the habit of misknowing, so we must make sure that we learn from authentic sources, and then we can feel confident of authentic experience and realization.

Now, although there are all sorts of different personalities and ideologies promoted as Buddhist and enlightened these days, unfortunately, not all of them are authentic. We have to take some care to ensure that a teacher, a text, and the teaching that they convey are from an unbroken lineage that can be traced back to the Buddha and that they present the teachings in a noncontradictory manner. In Tibet, we have what are known as the "eight chariots," or schools, from which the mainstream traditions developed, such as the Nyingma, Sakya, Kagyu, and Gelug, all of which synthesize the authentic teachings of the Buddha and later works from the great scholars of Nalanda University in India. Once we have the fortune to find authentic, learned, and experienced teachers, it is not enough just to seek quick blessings, like through lots of long-life empowerments. We must rely on their teachings of the meaning of the view in Buddhism, having taken plenty of time to examine their qualities, and then integrate those teachings into our everyday life so that we can bring about actual transformation. On the basis of sound morality, we develop an understanding of the right view through authentic and prolific learning. Even if we are unable to attend many teachings or to study a lot, we still can make sure to receive some teachings on the most important texts, such as *Entering the Bodhisattva's Way of Life*, and to remember some of the powerful verses in it to remind us of the right view, meditation, and conduct throughout our lives. This will really help us find greater calm, clarity, and insight.

Wisdom

When we have the richness of learning, we contemplate and meditate, and this leads us to the other topic: wisdom. In order for our wisdom to be really rich, it has to be more than just intellectual knowledge or knowledge about various topics; it's a transcendental understanding of truth, and that knowing of truth is liberating. In order to achieve a nonconceptual knowing that is beyond mere beliefs or views, we have to abide in a deep tranquility that allows the defilements that hinder our clarity and our ability to discern reality to fade away. This is achieved through what we call *dhyana* (deep meditative states), which in turn we reach through the stages of *shamatha*, or calm-abiding meditation. We call the meditation that develops wisdom *vipashyana*, which means "special insight." Ordinary insight is into particular ordinary topics, like "Oh, I have insight now with the settings on the TV so I can change it back after I've played on my games console without my tutors knowing!" It is when we achieve calm-abiding meditation, which we learn from authentic meditation masters, that our clarity of mind is razor-sharp and at least temporarily free from defilements, so it becomes special—special insight. The richest wisdom is the wisdom free from all blocks and any trace of personal interest; it is the wisdom of a buddha, and the seed for that is within us all. That is why the great Indian master Chandrakirti opened his commentary *Introduction to the*

Middle Way with the homage to great compassion, because to attain that richest wisdom, we need the great compassion that aspires to attain the stage of a buddha for the welfare of all wandering beings. We need the bow of compassion, the arrow of wisdom, and the archer of skillful means. That skillful means integrates wisdom and compassion.

Through developing calm-abiding meditation and special insight meditation in unison, as Dharmakirti said in his *Commentary on Epistemology*:

> Since the net of conceptual thinking is ripped apart, we see with inherent clarity.

We have to feel confident that we can achieve this, apply ourselves with enthusiasm to our Dharma practice, and not think that wisdom is more important than merit or that merit is more important than wisdom. If we practice an integrated approach, we will be able to traverse the five paths and ten levels that a bodhisattva goes through to realize our ultimate wisdom and bring optimum benefit to our world.

Discovery

This prospect might seem a very grand thing right now. We might think, "How can an ordinary person like me attain such noble qualities?" But remember, even the most famous Tibetan masters such as Milarepa started off as ordinary practitioners, yet through their joyful devotion to the practice, they became realized aryans. So, no matter where we come from, whatever our gender or background, if we too develop the riches of faith, charity, morality, personal conscience, social conscience, learning, and wisdom, then we too can become realized aryans. Then our lives will not have been wasted.

Even if you don't have one dollar in your pocket, you will still be rich beyond your wildest dreams.

3

The Miracle of Awakening

Recently, I was asked about a particular Vajrayana practice focused on meditating on a female enlightened form that can help us connect the seven limbs of bodhi in this and every lifetime in order to reach the stage of a perfectly complete Buddha.

In reply to the request, I mentioned that we must always be careful not to think of the enlightened form or deities that we meditate on in the Vajrayana as some kind of superior personality "out there" who poor humble not-good-enough little "me" needs to try to be like. The seed of the awakening is within *you*. Relating to all these different embodiments of the Buddha's qualities is a way of mirroring this amazing potential; to evoke wisdom, compassion, and strength from the inside. In other words, as far as I'm concerned, you're already awesome–and don't you forget it.

What Are the "Limbs of Bodhi"?

What are the so-called seven limbs of bodhi? Bodhi is–well, bodhi. Mostly, people say "enlightenment" in English, but I don't favor that translation. I researched this, and the root Sanskrit syllable *bodh* has three connotations. One is to have cleared away, one is to perfectly complete something, and one is simply to awaken. I don't think any of them are really conveyed by the English word *enlightenment*. In Tibetan, we say *jangchub*. *Jang* means to have cleared away all afflictions, and *chub* means to have perfectly completed the qualities of realization. Put them together and *jangchub* conveys the sense of the awakened state—the state in which all afflictive and cognitive obscurations have been purified, the two accumulations of merit and wisdom have been completely perfected, and one has awakened the dual knowing of things as they are and things in their extent. As for the limbs, although it's not incorrect to say "factor" or something like that, and perhaps "limb" sounds a bit odd, I like it. In ordinary terms, the limbs together are what animates the human body—it's so much more dynamic than just saying "factor" or "component." And together, these extraordinary limbs are what bring the realized aryan to life on the path of seeing, the first level of awakening for bodhisattvas.

The Primary Importance of the Seven Limbs

These seven limbs of bodhi are included as the twenty-third to the twenty-ninth of thirty-seven factors that are conducive to bodhi. Sorry to give you all these numbers to remember, but they have a good purpose. In fact, this particular set—the enumeration of Dharma called the thirty-seven factors conducive to bodhi—is not just a key teaching in the Pali Canon traditions of early Buddhism; it's an indispensable teaching for bodhisattvas relying on the Mahayana sutras too.

Enumerations of Dharma are helpful as a mnemonic device to firmly implant these topics in our brains for contemplation and meditation, but in a way that's easy for our minds to access the actual deeper meanings we've learned. And then the important thing is not just to memorize long lists of subject headings but to study their meanings, contemplate them, and penetrate them in meditation.

In a prayer by the Tibetan master Sakya Pandita, the Buddha is praised like this:

> Mindfulness, joyful vigor, *samadhi* (deep meditation),
> The wondrous faculties and strengths,
> The limbs of bodhi, and the aryan path:
>> To you who fully accomplished them I offer
>> homage.

Sakya Pandita was saying that what makes the Buddha a buddha is that he has fully accomplished these thirty-seven factors without anything remaining. So, if we are serious about making our aspiring and engaging bodhichitta—the altruistic determination for full awakening—more than words, we better take a closer look at those seven magic numbers that we need to play in the miracle lottery ticket for bodhi.

Foundations

First, we need to be clear about our objective. It is said that the seven limbs are so powerful that just from hearing about them, healing and peace can arise. But any of the thirty-seven limbs of bodhi must be directed at the four noble truths in the development of special insight to qualify as a real Buddhist pursuit. The four truths refer to suffering, the source of suffering, the cessation of suffering, and the path. We accrue the two accumulations of merit and wisdom, accompanied by definitive letting go, which accumulates the causes of liberation, and develop bodhichitta to accumulate the causes of bodhi. If definitive letting go is present without bodhichitta, it qualifies as the practice aimed at personal liberation but not complete bodhi. If both definitive letting go and bodhichitta are present, it qualifies as the bodhisattvas' practice of the Mahayana. We need to be fully conscious of this, because when the right view in our practice is married to the right actions—committing to moral conduct, abandoning all distractions, and so on—then our meditation can really live happily ever after.

Just to explore the foundations briefly in essence: all practitioners must meditate on suffering, impermanence, and selflessness. When the goal of practice is personal liberation alone, the meditation on selflessness only focuses on the personality, the lack of an inherent unchanging identity. But in the Mahayana, although we start with that, we also target the selflessness of all apparent phenomena. The general result is that the four objects of reference are done away with and the special result is that one transcends the five aggregates that make up the sense of self—form, feeling, perception, formatives, and consciousness—together with their resultant experiences.

Now, that higher view is really important because each of the limbs is preceded by the word *right*, such as the bodhi-limb of right mindfulness and so on. This doesn't just mean right as in doctrinally correct, conforming to what's written in scriptures or from what scholars have said—although if our experience aligns with what they say, then sure, that's a nice pat on the back. They're right when they are pure through the elimination of wrong view.

The Bodhi Limb of Right Mindfulness

Of the seven limbs, first we have the bodhi limb of right mindfulness. I think *mindfulness* is a word that's quite fashionable right now. There's a kind of vogue I hear a lot about these days for something that resembles Buddhist mindfulness, only without the moral precepts, without bodhichitta, and, well, without anything even close to aiming at true liberation or enlightenment. I don't want to disparage something that may well be helping people with their stress or whatever, but I just feel a bit uncomfortable that a lot of people think that this alone is the essence of what all Buddhism is about. The right mindfulness that we're interested in is mainly practiced on the basis of the right foundations through what are called the four close placements: of body, feelings, mind, and topics. Cultivating them accumulates wisdom; the accompanying motivation accumulates merit. They reinforce each other.

I think that what's been hijacked by the commercialized secular mindfulness fads is more the Buddhists' presentation of mindfulness that is aimed only at personal liberation as a kind of foundation for the calm-abiding meditation that the monks in that tradition do, always applying their attention to the breath. Although in-and-out breathing is neutral in itself, such Buddhist systems only teach this in the context of established virtue, like refraining from what's unwholesome as explained in the *vinaya*, the monastic code of conduct. How we generally present it in the Mahayana, as clarified by the fourth-century Indian brothers Vasubandhu and Asanga as well as others, is that right mindfulness is a universal mental factor of consciousness that adds noting to it, allowing for later recollection. This doesn't mean just noting like the ordinary voice in our head chatting away behind what we're doing; it's more an intuitive perception of what we would usually ignore if we weren't being heedful. This means recollecting an object that is a virtuous awareness, which understands its object. In other words, it's not just a spacy nonjudging that we label afterward as being "in the moment" so that worries don't surface to disturb us too much. It's a full commitment of consciousness in the here and now that has the real confidence, resolve, and wisdom behind it to directly face suffering, its source, and so forth.

Now, if we want to penetrate the meaning of the four truths, how do we do that? In the close placement of mindfulness of body, we penetrate the truth of suffering; for that, we awaken understanding by finely analyzing the suffering of the body formative. In the close placement of mindfulness of feeling, we penetrate the truth of the source of suffering; for that, we understand that painful, pleasant, and neutral feelings all have a cause, the principal source being craving. In the close placement of mindfulness of mind, we penetrate the truth of cessation; for that, by instant consciousness apart from identification from that cessation, we actualize the end of suffering. In the close placement of mindfulness of topics, we penetrate the truth of the path; for that, we realize the abandonment of the phenomena of passion and the other afflictions, and we make the phenomena of faith and the other purifying qualities really firm.

Mindfulness as a limb of bodhi is called the limb of abiding—mindfulness of what is virtuous so our minds can focus on the four truths. It's what will bring us victory over our troubles by bringing us the understanding of what we haven't yet really understood. Mindfulness as a practice, side by side with vigilance, is simple. Simple, but not easy. Although I want to be clear about its definition, I don't want to make it complicated, like something exotic we have to try to acquire. It's a direct putting-into-practice, a natural flowering of our buddha nature. In other words, as we live with this fullness of awareness in our lives on the path of accumulation, it's like a glimpse of the knowing that we'll discover on the path of seeing.

The Bodhi Limb of Right Discernment of Phenomena

Second, we have fine discernment of phenomena, which is the limb of the essence. In the Mahayana, we have the five paths that bodhisattvas work tirelessly to traverse to reach the stage of a complete buddha in order to benefit all sentient beings. As our practice begins, we create the causes of the path of accumulation. When we are no longer wannabe bodhisattvas but have our first real realization of voidness, we are official aryans on the path of seeing reality as it is. The path of connection is the bridge between those two. After the path of seeing, we have the path of meditation—not ordinary meditation, but a great bodhisattva's meditation—and finally the path of no more learning, which is when bodhisattvas advance to become buddhas. On the basis of our mindfulness, which presents the labeled forms of appearances in consciousness, right discernment of these phenomena overcomes all adversity by overcoming incorrect self-grasping thoughts of person and phenomena, self and other. For this, the path of seeing is awakened in the nature of wisdom.

The Bodhi Limb of Right Joyful Vigor

This pursuit is no part-time hobby. Our mindfulness and discernment inspire the third limb, right joyful vigor, which is the limb of letting go. This is the drive to enthusiastically apply ourselves 24/7, no matter how long it takes, to bring about the swift accomplishment of the ultimate qualities we long for.

Now, this is amazing—think about it: the Buddha equates applying effort to letting go. Our ordinary goal-oriented way of thinking would consider these two totally different approaches. The thing is, when we have that vision of reality, when we see that what we've been clinging to all this time as "me" and what should make "me" happy through the senses is like a bad joke, then we stop playing the game. We let it go. That is such a relief. It opens up a whole field of energy that has until now been tied up and wasted on useless stuff. It's like breaking a dam and all the water just rushes out. So joyful vigor is not about beating ourselves up that we're not trying hard enough and *push, push, push!*

> "Now, look! I don't care if Netflix has released a whole new series you've been waiting for in one day. You can't enjoy such things! Not even one episode! Get back on your cushion and do your meditation or you're not trying hard enough!"

> "Sir, yes, sir!!"

No, it's more like this:

> "What am I doing wasting my energy getting caught up in all this illusory drama of shoulds and shouldn'ts? This *samsara*—this

cyclical existence in suffering—is the worst sci-fi ever! How about I let all that go? Is that so bad? No, it's awesome!"

The Bodhi Limb of Right Rapture

When we tap into that vast resource of energy, it's great, but these bodhisattvas must get really tired and irritable helping sentient beings all the time, huh? Nope. Not according to the Buddha. He said that the fourth limb of bodhi that comes from all this mindfulness, discernment, and effort is actually joy or rapture, and this is the limb of the advantage or benefit from such practice. It's the complete opposite of what happens when we operate from the selfish worldly mind. Normally, it'd be like this:

"Hey, dude, c'mon. There's a special event downtown today to raise money for the homeless. Wanna come and help?"

"Um, yeah, about that... I *would*. It's just that I'm on the final episode of the latest season of *Game of Thrones* here, and I've *gotta* see how it ends. Another time...."

So yes, there is that constant pursuit of the next hit of pleasure for the senses to come in the future... but when we truly live in the present moment and the mind stream is satisfied, why would we chase something fleeting outside?

The bodhisattva's rapture is not so much a feeling in the regular sense; it's an internal meditative experience beyond the senses. It's not a personal thing that "I" have to try to get. It's a natural state that's already here, and we discover it when we're no longer craving something else through the senses. The present-moment felt sense of body and mind—all of it is completely suffused with a beautiful joy that is so much richer than anything that can tingle the senses for a moment or two. How much more we can do with our time, our lives, our goals, when we awaken the bodhisattvas' rapture rather than coping with the mood swings that delusions give us.

The Bodhi Limb of Right Pliancy

This brings us to the fifth limb, which we can call "right pliancy." It's the limb of the mind being made so peaceful and workable that none of the afflictions are agitated in relation to anything, because their causes, which are the different negativities, are subdued. This enables the mind to clearly apprehend its object in meditation. You know, everyone says they want world peace . . . but do we really? Really? I mean, if we look around and there's nothing special going on, what do we do with that peace? Is it joyful? Or does it give room to disturbing thoughts and feelings that we normally don't notice in the busyness of our daily lives?

> "Remember that time you tried telling that joke and no one laughed? Whoa, so embarrassing! Or that time your best friend said he was disappointed with you. Man! That stings. Don't wanna think about that. Makes my jaw clench and my shoulders tighten. Um, better check WhatsApp and play a game on my phone instead. . . ."

Now, how can we say we want world peace if our peace is like an unsettling empty room? That's not peace—that's boredom! But when the causes aren't there, when afflictive emotions are replaced with virtuous qualities, then peace is not uncomfortable, it's full—a huge room full of joy, full of light, full of beauty. Now that is the kind of peace that we can share with the world.

The Bodhi Limb of Right Samadhi

A pliant and peaceful body and mind creates the perfect potential to naturally transfuse into abiding in the sixth limb, the limb of right samadhi (for which there's no one word in English, but it refers to the deep meditation taught by the Buddha). *Samadhi* literally means "holding to the deep." It is the full meditative state in which, at least while one is in it, the afflictive emotional obscurations are not active.

The Buddha never taught the development of calm abiding as separate from the development of special insight. They have to be conjoined in order to fulfill our wishes. When we allow the mind to be truly stable, unafflicted, intensely blissful, concentrated, and collected in a state of samadhi, we purify the mind so that the wisdom that directly perceives voidness can manifest. If we don't cultivate the factors for such deep meditation because we're caught up in worldly affairs that breed attachment, unable to enjoy solitude, and so forth, then how can we expect to experience the esoteric meditative states such as the luminescence of the special teachings of *dzogrim* or *dzogchen*? Come on, that's just wishful thinking! It's like becoming the world's leading expert on chocolate—dark chocolate, milk chocolate, white chocolate, Swiss chocolate, Belgian chocolate, chocolate using beans from the Amazon, chocolate using beans from sub-Saharan Africa—but without ever having tried even one mouthful. However, if we learn how to cultivate samadhi from a qualified teacher—since we can't do it just from books—then we will learn how to taste all the flavors of the most delicious attainments, both worldly and transcendent, that we could ever wish for.

The Bodhi Limb of Right Equanimity

From learning the stages of such transformative mental development, we will discover the final limb, which is the essence of not being afflicted in any way, the limb of right equanimity beyond any fluctuation of dullness or agitation, beyond any concepts, beyond any need to even try.

Even for an ordinary practitioner who is not yet an aryan bodhisattva, a temporary experience in meditation without afflictive emotions is a taste of what will definitely follow the paths to the ultimate freedom; as this blossoms, we will abide in the very cure for all obstacles inside and outside our meditation sessions.

How the Limbs Are Cultivated

To sum up, in considering the truth of suffering, we seek out the solitudes of body and so on and abide with the truth of suffering. Considering the truth of the source, we wish to part from it. Considering the truth of cessation, we wish to bring about direct perception. Considering the truth of the path, we wish to discard afflictions. Our practice of the seven limbs elevates them from being considerations to being meditations—meditations that will awaken.

Our practice of the seven limbs will awaken the mind without the four inversions, the knowing mind with which we will traverse all the levels and paths to the stage of a perfectly complete buddha in order to benefit all wandering beings. And in order to do this, we have practices in the Vajrayana in which we meditate on all the buddhas and bodhisattvas of the three times and ten directions to connect us with the seven limbs until we reach the very same stage as the enlightened ones.

4

The Cause for Attaining Everything on the Path

To possess aspiring bodhichitta, the altruistic intent for full awakening to benefit all beings, is what defines a follower of Mahayana Buddhism. Refuge and bodhichitta are the indispensable preliminaries for every practice in our tradition. That is why we meditate on refuge and bodhichitta at the beginning of all our meditation practices.

What is our refuge? That is, of course, the Triple Gem: the Buddha, the Dharma, and the spiritual community of the Sangha. Bodhichitta is the mind of great compassion that wishes for all sentient beings to attain the stage of a completely perfect buddha; without this, we can't ever attain awakening, bodhi. Even if we can't practice many things, if we can practice bodhichitta, as the great scholar Nagarjuna explained in his *Letter to the King*, we can attain everything that we aspire on the path.

The Causes of Bodhichitta

So how do we make this idea we call *bodhichitta* really come to life?

First, we need love. Not just like, "I love ice cream" or "I love the new ride at Disney World," but really strong love from the very depths of our hearts. This love is not just for the people who are easy to love, like our mom, our buddies, and so on. It's the deep love for all the sentient beings who have been our dear mothers in countless previous lives, without any bias or exceptions. We wish for all of them as well as ourselves to have happiness and the causes of happiness. And we wish them to be safe, free from all suffering, stress, and pain. That is compassion.

Then there is a foundation for love and compassion as a cause of bodhichitta, and that is the meditation on the intrinsic suffering of unenlightened existence (samsara), the endless cycle of suffering. In the Buddhist sutras, it says that understanding the nature of existence in samsara to be dissatisfactory is like a spring and understanding love and compassion for those who undergo suffering in samsara is like the river issuing out of that spring.

The Conditions That Strengthen Bodhichitta

If love and compassion, on the basis of seeing the inherent suffering of existence in samsara, are the causes, what are the conditions that help make bodhichitta something we can really feel, something we can really work with? There are seven conditions for that.

The first is to rely on an authentic teacher, to really feel faith and to really trust from the bottom of our hearts the qualified guide who inspires us.

The second is to have really strong devotion in the Triple Gem. In Buddhism, we don't just believe out of blind faith, but we feel confidence in our objects of refuge for reasons. So our strong devotion in the Triple Gem must come from the three types of faith described in the teachings—admiring faith, aspirational faith, and the faith of full conviction.

The third is to study the teachings to see what the degrading misdeeds are; then, once we see that for ourselves, we make a strong determination not to commit them in the future.

The fourth is to offer prayers to the buddhas and bodhisattvas that we will not fall into bad ways. For the third and the fourth, it also helps if we often do purification practices, such as Vajrasattva in which we sincerely express regret for any negative things we did with our body, speech, or mind. We also need to think about the suffering that comes from degrading misdeeds to help us avoid them and to avoid developing unhealthy habits.

The fifth is to contemplate. We reflect on all the positive aspects of bodhichitta, and then we reflect on all the negative aspects of un-enlightened existence and even the limitations of personal liberation alone. If we contemplate the limitations of practicing solely for the sake of personal liberation rather than universal liberation, this also steers us away from being too obsessed with the idea of voidness to escape from our own suffering, which is something of a danger for bodhisattvas. But we also don't want to make ourselves feel down with too much thinking about the suffering of samsara and so on, so we must balance this with remembering that human life is so precious and that we want to make it really meaningful and beautiful. We become determined that we *will* do this.

The sixth is to remember all the excellent qualities of the bud-dhas and bodhisattvas before us who have nurtured bodhichitta through such qualities as their ability to produce many manifesta-tions that work for the welfare of others, their many extraordinary abilities, and so forth. We pray to our spiritual guide as the one who embodies the body, speech, mind, qualities, and activities of all the Enlightened Ones, buddhas, and bodhisattvas so that we may quickly attain these excellent qualities and receive all the temporal and ulti-mate benefits of bodhichitta in this very life.

Finally, the seventh is our own inspiration, our enthusiasm to work for the welfare of all sentient beings, which includes our-selves.

With these seven practices, we can really turn on the light of bodhichitta, and we can make that light very strong.

The reason I am describing all this is also so that when we have strong bodhichitta, good conditions will naturally increase and we can naturally reduce the obstacles to our goal.

Obstacles to Bodhichitta

We need to know what the main obstacles to bodhichitta are. First, if there is any bad attitude, such as any negative thinking or lack of real respect for the spiritual guide or Triple Gem, it will cause bodhichitta to degenerate.

If we don't overcome selfish ways, if we still put our own interests and happiness before others, and if we have any jealousy about others' good fortune and qualities, this is also the cause of degeneration.

Other things we need to avoid are thinking that we don't need to develop bodhichitta in a gradual way according to the teachings of the great masters but have a kind of pride that makes us think we can just do some shortcut practice or leap straight into esoteric practices like dzogchen or something like that. That can be an obstacle because then we're not really thinking about the excellent qualities of the buddhas and bodhisattvas and trying to achieve those excellent qualities ourselves in the right way.

Antidotes to the Obstacles to Bodhichitta

If we practice the seven conditions that make bodhichitta strong, then we won't fall prey to these obstacles. We must not allow discouragement to creep into our minds but feel inspiration and self-confidence. We are all the same human beings, no matter what our background, gender, age, and so forth. We all have the same potential. I think everyone is very special in their own way. We can all be very intelligent and kind. So since the mind is very powerful, we must make our minds strong with self-confidence and not let thoughts of doubt, low self-esteem, or depression overwhelm us.

We might also see some of the very bad things happening in the world, such as mass murders and other terrible actions committed by very bad people, or the conditions in very poor countries where there is so much starvation and sickness, and then get discouraged thinking, "How can I, just one person meditating on bodhichitta, make a difference when there is so much unbearable suffering going on?" However, if we think deeper, this is just the suffering we can see in the human world; this does not include the suffering of the lower realms, which are much, much bigger. So we must think, "No matter how many sentient beings there are, no matter how much suffering there is, every one of them is like my only beloved child, and I will do whatever it takes, no matter what, to take their suffering away."

It also helps if we remember that, if we carefully analyze it, all that makes up phenomena appears in terms of the five aggregates (form, feeling, perception, formatives, and consciousness) and is like an illusion and, on that basis, since the three times (past, present, and future) are as though without a beginning or end, there's no real difference between a whole eon and a single instant here and now. We must also remember the exemplary compassion of the spiritual guides who teach the Dharma for universal liberation without ever tiring from benefiting others, and never fail to put our energy into the cultivation of bodhichitta.

The Results of Bodhichitta

Moreover, we can't think that if we practice bodhichitta, then that is something that only brings results very far ahead in future lives. Actually, if we practice bodhichitta, it will bring results not only in the future but also in this life too, such as more happiness, health, abundance, and so forth. This relates to our karma—the law of cause and effect in terms of our intentional actions by body, speech, and mind, and the corresponding results that we experience.

Karma is quite an in-depth topic in Buddhist philosophy, but basically it is explained that actions, whether good, bad, or neutral, can bring results in this life, in the next life, or after a number of rebirths. If the results of karma are to ripen more in this life than further in the future, then we need very strong intention, action, and object of action. In that case, what stronger, what better practice than bodhichitta to bring us benefits for this and future lives?

5
Putting Aspiration into Action

On the basis of aspiring bodhichitta, we can practice engaging bodhichitta, which means the actual practice of the bodhisattvas, like the bodhisattva of wisdom Manjushri, who is a beloved figure of spiritual inspiration in our tradition. There are different ways of describing this, but the main way is the six transcendent perfections, the *paramitas*. The sixth of these is wisdom, but as it is taught, without joining with wisdom, the other five practices, although they are still virtuous, are not transcendent perfections—so cultivating wisdom is vital on the bodhisattva path. So what are the six transcendent perfections?

Generosity

The first is generosity. The great Tibetan Buddhist teacher Sakya Pandita explained that this means using something of value to help others. It is the opposite of being selfish. We cultivate generosity through the three types of giving: giving material things, giving fearlessness, and giving the Dharma. Sometimes we add a fourth to that list, which is giving love.

At first, it might be hard to give many things. As Shantideva says in *Entering the Bodhisattva's Way of Life*, we can start by offering small things that we can all afford, like fruits and things like that, and eventually, with practice, we will be able to be like the great bodhisattva who gave his own limbs to feed a starving tigress. In Buddhism, the mind is most important, so we can all cultivate generosity through meditation and then through action as well.

Morality

The second transcendent perfection is morality, which Sakya Pandita said is avoiding unwholesome behavior for the welfare of others. We can practice this by refraining from the ten unvirtuous deeds: no killing, stealing, or sexual misconduct; no deceitful, divisive, senseless, or abusive speech; and no covetousness, ill will, or wrong views in the mind.

Whether we keep the vows of a layperson, the vows of a novice, or the vows of a nun or monk, these ten trainings are something like the foundation for all of us. However, although we all try very hard, sometimes we may do, say, or think something that we see is wrong afterward, so then it's good if we purify past degrading misdeeds through practices such as those taught in the *Three Heap Sutra*, or the Vajrasattva practice, and other such purifying practices. If we also study the teachings on karma and dependent origination, then this will help us to understand why morality is so important for our Dharma practice.

Patience

The third is patience, which is not being agitated when harmed by others. With patience, we can overcome anger, which is the greatest disturbance to our mind and our happiness in this life and all our future lives too.

We must treat others as we want to be treated, even if we face obstacles and negativity. We have to transform problems through patience and in that way grow in our practice. Then we can generate a field of positive energy around us that keeps helping us and encouraging others.

Anger disempowers our mind; it kind of spoils our power of intentionality and discernment. But patience empowers our responsiveness and our intelligence.

Sometimes, we might think we can't really practice patience, and when we experience something very upsetting, we might say "I just can't bear it anymore!" but if we really analyze with reasoning, then we can develop inner strength to accept some sufferings that we can't change at first and then to overcome the problems that we can change. The more we develop our understanding of Dharma, especially the true nature of mind and appearances, eventually we will develop the ultimate patience that won't be disturbed by anything, good or bad.

Joyful Vigor

The fourth transcendent perfection is sometimes called "effort" or "diligence," but I don't think those words show the real meaning of this one. It means an inspiration, a kind of joy that comes with wanting to practice Dharma for the sake of others. So I call it "joyful vigor." If we have this joyful vigor, then we will get rid of depression and laziness and the couch-potato mind.

For this, it is good to have a passion for a happy life, because when we combine this with wisdom, it gives us the momentum to practice Dharma and help others to have a happy life too.

Often we waste so much energy through stress, worry, anxiety, and excessive thinking around a negative self-image or even other people's problems. But I noticed that in our monasteries in India, the Sanghas have to work really hard and we're always busy studying, but generally we are calm and happy and have more energy because of Dharma practice—I mean because of joyful vigor.

We have to channel our determination by recognizing our capacity, and what our limits are and what our positive qualities are, through wise reflection. I find it helpful to remember that the body is, by nature, limited. I mean, we all get sick sometimes and stuff like that, but the mind's potential is limitless and, by nature, pure, so we must take strength from this and not feel down. So how can we really do that?

Meditation

This leads to the fifth transcendent perfection. There's no direct translation of this word—in Sanskrit it's *dhyana*—but it refers to a deep state of meditation in which the mind is very stable, very concentrated, very blissful, and so on. Sakya Pandita stated that it is complete evenness of mind in deep meditation aimed at attaining the stage of a buddha for the welfare of all sentient beings.

Developing the mind through meditation practice must be learned from an experienced teacher, so I won't go into this so much here. If you can, it's good to study *The Stages of Meditation* by Kamalashila. Just to say a few brief words: We can cultivate dhyana with an object such as a visualization of the Buddha, Tara, or any enlightened figure, which is a really good object for our minds, or we can simply meditate on a four-petaled blue flower or a ball of light, which can sharpen our awareness and uplift our minds. And we can also cultivate dhyana subjectively, like generating the four immeasurables, which are loving-kindness, compassion, empathetic joy, and equanimity. So we can do it objectively, taking a chosen meditation object; or subjectively, cultivating the state of mind itself.

If we think our mind is always distracted and we can't concentrate one-pointedly, we must not be discouraged, but we can stop for a few moments and send love out to others. We can generate compassion by thinking of something that moved us and then reflecting on it some more. Just from that small experience, little by little, we can eventually attain perfect dhyana. Most important is that we try as often as we can to meditate deeply on love and compassion; this, Sakya Pandita said, is the main meditation of the bodhisattvas.

Wisdom

Then, as I mentioned, we join these five practices to the transcendent perfection of wisdom. They are called the "transcendent perfections" because if we completely perfect them and practice them at all times, then we will transcend the division of what is samsara and what is nirvana, and we will attain our own welfare and others' welfare too.

When we are at the beginners' level of developing these transcendent perfections, we analyze the selflessness of the person or the selflessness of phenomena. Then eventually we can attain actual realization, which is transcending, something we experience beyond ordinary concepts. Then all that we do, all that we say, and what we think will be informed by this awakening to reality.

This wisdom, Sakya Pandita explained, is the realization that the basic nature of everything—what we take to be the self, as well as phenomena that appear—is voidness, which is beyond the four limiting extremes of existing, not existing at all, being both, or being neither. This is not worldly wisdom and not wrong wisdom, like that of non-Buddhist philosophy, and not the incomplete wisdom of those who have attained only personal liberation, none of which uses wisdom to attain the stage of a buddha out of great compassion. We need the real wisdom of Manjushri as explained in the *Sutra Establishing the Qualities of Noble Manjushri's Buddha Realm* and so on. This is the omniscience that is free from the two obscurations: the afflictive obscurations, which are the roots of anger and so on, and the cognitive obscurations, which are the roots of confused dualistic thinking.

In modern times, Sakya Pandita pointed out, there are butchers selling donkey meat as real beef, which means there are people who call their teachings Buddhist philosophy, and even though they might look like good teachers, it's some made-up kind of thing. So it is really important to find authentic teachings from the authentic teachers to study the deep meaning of the wisdom of voidness in Buddhism.

Then we ourselves must investigate, through wise reflection, the causes and conditions for our happiness and suffering: "How do they arise?" "How do they feel?" "How do they pass?" and so on.

We then have faith and trust that we can evolve the deeper wisdom beyond those changing conditions according to the explanations of the great masters, such as the great Sakya Pandita.

In order to do this, we need the "three wheels," which are, first, study, then contemplation, and finally, meditation; and we need to cultivate the three wheels over a long time. It is excellent if we can study the major classic texts on wisdom, such as those by Nagarjuna, Shantideva, and the rest of the great Buddhist masters throughout history. But if that is difficult, at least we can try to receive essence teachings from experienced scholars. This can transform our whole life, and then our wisdom will inform every practice we do and everything we do in our day-to-day activities.

6

Transforming the Mind

Motivation

Please don't think of Dharma teachings as boring religious texts—I try my best not to bore you! Instead, think of them as an experiment for our everyday life. I'd like this experiment to prove successful, so I want to emphasize the practical side of the teachings for transforming our minds.

For this, it's important that we always pay careful attention to what our teachers say, so let's approach this as a precious opportunity to check how our practice is going and how much we're integrating the Dharma into our daily lives, not taking it casually or out of a feeling of obligation, thinking, "Oh, when will it be over?" What's important to keep in mind is what is being taught rather than the one who is teaching it, so we avoid the obstacle of thinking of ourselves as more qualified than the teacher. Think of the teacher as being something like a doctor and the teaching as like a medicine, and all our Dharma sisters and brothers as like the nurses supporting us, and we ourselves are like the patient.

The medicine of Dharma is not like temporary pain relief, like an aspirin. The Dharma is an ultimate tonic that cures all the afflictions.

So we're not focusing on just trying to make samsara a little bit more bearable, like just for short-term stress relief, nor are we focused on just our own escape from the afflictions. Rather, we're focusing our energy on how we can transform our minds for the ultimate welfare of all sentient beings.

What Is *Lojong,* or Mind Training?

I hope sharing this will motivate us to refresh our commitment to the bodhisattva's way of life and making the exchange practice–the exchange of our own well-being for the sufferings of others–our main practice. That is what my Dharma sharing is about: transforming the mind.

In Tibetan we call this *lojong,* which can be translated as mind training. There are different words for "mind" in Tibetan; the one here–*lo*–means our rational mind. It's like the way we think, our attitude maybe. It doesn't mean the way we feel as such, which would be *sem* in Tibetan. The key here is that we can not only train but totally turn around or transform the way we think, and this has a powerful effect on the way we feel. So through this mind training, we can transform the way we think and thereby the way we feel, and so bring about our own and others' true welfare.

The Basis of Transforming the Mind

We might have developed this habit of low self-esteem where we tend to get caught up in depression, anxiety, stress, feeling disempowered, frustrated, thinking, "Ugh, how can I really get over these issues? This is just how my life is. I'm so stressed." Then we're trapped in the cage of afflictive emotions without realizing that the key is hanging on the wall right in front of us. So, what is the way out? We don't just prostrate to that key or meditate on its ultimate nature or whatever–all we have to do is turn the key and unlock the door.

What I mean is that, actually, the basic nature of mind, according to the Buddha, is pure, like the lotus flower. Even though lotuses grow in swamps and muddy ponds, they always blossom without any dirt on them. In the same way, the afflictive emotions are like temporary stains, but the mind can always rise above them without any contamination.

The problem is that we forget this. We get caught up in our afflictive emotions, and then we cling to a negative sense of self and others. From this, we tend to react, and that is how karma works. If we're caught up in our feelings, then we're letting ourselves be controlled by them, so we can't think straight, and all kinds of karma plays out. This is the vicious circle of endless suffering and stress. If we cultivate more mindfulness and inner vigilance to be *with* our feelings instead of being caught up *in* them, then we are more empowered to respond instead of react; we're taking back control of our lives and our sense of freedom. That enables us to reflect and see that what stresses us out a lot of the time is just appearances on the inner TV screen of our minds. It's like a TV series with all the different characters and plots, but we must not believe in it too much and attach to it, but to see it as just appearances and let go.

The Essence of the Bodhisattva Vow

As I mentioned, this book is designed for those who practice the Mahayana, which is the vehicle of the bodhisattvas. The essence of this is that those who practice it can't bear to see their loved ones in pain; they can't bear the suffering in the world, and they feel a great responsibility to do something about it in order to bring them to the end of all suffering. How can that be done? Worldly deities can't do it; those who have attained only personal liberation can't either. Only the completely perfect Buddha has realized the full potential to pull them out of the ocean of samsara. So we do whatever it takes to reach the stage of a buddha for the sake of all sentient beings. The essence of this endeavor in relation to transforming the mind is that we have to exchange our merit and happiness for the pain and suffering of others.

I already explained that our motivation is compassion, the actual practice that we're learning is compassion, and the result is also compassion, so that is why this teaching is so very precious. I think that without this attitude in our hearts, it will be very hard to really achieve much from our Dharma practice. Even if we tried to do many advanced techniques without it, they wouldn't be very effective. But if we cultivate bodhichitta from the depths of our hearts as our main practice, then even the most advanced practices will be effective and go very smoothly. So the exchange practice is the most essential practice for us—it's like the life blood of the path. Any amount of study, contemplation, and meditation we do on the exchange practice will be of immense benefit.

The root of this is to cherish all sentient beings dearly, without any discrimination. We cannot harbor the mind that discriminates, which leads to degrading misdeeds such as oppressing and being violent toward women or being cruel to people of other races just because of how they look. Regardless of a person's weight, race, gender, sexual orientation, cultural background, and so forth, we are all the same. Even other animals—dogs, cats, or cows—just because they are not as intelligent as humans does not mean that we should treat them badly. I'm not saying to treat them exactly the same as humans—that's a different story—but just to treat them kindly. However, we should treat all humans with equal respect; we must cherish them, help them, and be kind to them as much as possible out of compassion, without any of those discriminations.

There are different classic texts that explain how to do mind training, but I have chosen one that I have found very helpful for my own practice. Although it's very short—just eight verses—I feel that the whole Mahayana path is contained in its essence. We can easily recite it every day.

May I Always Hold Sentient Beings Dear

The first verse reads:

> For me, all sentient beings
> Are more special than a wish-fulfilling jewel,
> So with the intention to accomplish their optimum
>   welfare,
> May I always hold them dear.

This means that if you obtained a wish-fulfilling jewel, and then you polished it and put it on top of a victory banner and prayed to it, you could have all that you want. That could bring you a lifetime's supply of ice cream or a cool sports car or a billion dollars or a giant palace in Hawaii next to the beach or whatever. Or you could wish for something nobler perhaps, like world peace and for all war to end, or for all poverty to end, and things like that. However, even if we had all that and more, it still could not bring us the real end of suffering, nor could it bring us to the stage of a buddha. But all sentient beings can actually fulfill not only our ordinary wishes but our ultimate goals too, because by working for their welfare, we build up the accumulations of merit and wisdom necessary to overcome the two obscurations. How can we cultivate the two accumulations—specifically through the six transcendent perfections—without sentient beings? Who would we be generous toward? Who would we practice patience with? If we think of it in that way, we will see that sentient beings are more precious than anything in this world.

For ordinary worldly people, though, the habit is to think of number one—me, me, me. And there is a reason for this. It's only natural that we all want to be happy and free from suffering. We cherish ourselves, but we never achieve all our goals, and then we never feel truly fulfilled and only compound our suffering as a result. As Shantideva said, "All suffering in the universe comes from self-cherishing; all happiness comes from cherishing others."

So we must learn to see all sentient beings as very precious. If we use the special faculty of our human intelligence, then we can reason that by cherishing others' welfare above our own narrow desires, the benefits go both ways.

For instance, when we are more loving and caring toward others, they will naturally feel more comfortable in our company; they will think us more trustworthy and say complimentary things about us. Moreover, we will feel better about ourselves and our life. Having a loving heart will mean that we are more patient with sentient beings. Then, as we are calmer, our blood pressure will probably not be too high, so then even our health will be better. Those are the temporary benefits. The ultimate benefit is that, through practicing the six transcendent perfections, we will attain the stage of a buddha. When we think of it that way, what more could we possibly ask for?

Now reflect on the meaning of the last line of the first verse: May I always hold [sentient beings] dear.

May I Hold Others Supreme

Right now, we're not thinking in terms of a mega-long retreat hidden away in a cave in the Himalayas or the deep jungle or wherever, away from civilization. That's for another day. Even Milarepa, one of Tibet's greatest yogis, had to come down from the mountains and teach people eventually. For now we're thinking of our practice in relation to the people around us in our everyday lives. And the reality is that not everyone we meet is going to be like His Holiness the Dalai Lama or Mother Teresa. In my own life, most of the people around me are so nice and caring; it's very rare for me to meet people who are cruel or nasty. When I'm in the temples, for example, because of my position in the Tibetan Buddhist community, and I guess because I try to be nice to everyone, everyone shows me such kindness and goodwill, so it's really quite easy for me to be patient and compassionate. But then, even though it's rare, I can't have it like that all the time, and that's good or I'd never really practice what I preach.

Not so long ago, I was on a journey, checking in at a very busy airport. To cut a long story short, I muddled up our passports, so at passport control, one of the managers called me over and really scolded me like I was some kind of idiot. I was quite shocked and felt humiliated, as he did it in front of everyone. I guess it was all the more potent because I wasn't used to it. But, you know, I thought straightaway, "Avi, this is the perfect time to practice!" This taste of reality really gave me some idea of why the teachings emphasize so much that we need sentient beings in order to develop our spiritual path. If we try to hide away, thinking, "Oh, these people are so annoying! Why can't they leave me in peace to do *real* Dharma practice?" then we can fall into that trap, and then we will never become buddhas. So everyone who comes into our lives, no matter what their needs, issues, looks, expectations, or whatever, is giving us a wonderful chance to accelerate our practice.

This means that the heart of our exchange practice, on the basis of compassion, is to always put others before ourselves. But I want to make an important point here. The root of all our suffering is the mind of self-grasping, but this does not mean that we should beat ourselves up and get mired in low self-esteem—not at all.

Understanding selflessness does not mean that we should foster a negative self-image. That's still self-grasping. One form of it is the other extreme of narcissism, thinking that because of your looks or your skills or your worldly achievements or your learning or your race or your gender or your charisma or whatever, somehow you are better than everyone else. That's one type of grasping at a sense of self that doesn't understand that what we take to be "I" is really just composed of impermanent factors, like the various limbs of our physical form, the memories and feelings of our psychological makeup, and so forth. The other extreme is the opposite: "Oh, I'm such a loser. Why can't I get out of this dark cloud of despair? Why do I feel so insecure all the time? Oh, God!"

Of course, if we're arrogantly selfish, then we'll have a long, lonely life with only self-grasping as our friend, and he will always take us in the opposite direction of bodhichitta. If we're forever beating ourselves up, we will never have the confidence, courage, and conviction to cultivate compassion. So actually, we need really strong confidence, courage, and conviction to be able to put others before ourselves. If we have this inner strength, then we will be strong enough to realize that self-grasping of any kind is like carrying a ticking time bomb, and we will act from that realization by working for the welfare of others.

Try to reflect every day, not just in meditation but wherever you are—office, park, bathroom, wherever—on the meaning of this second verse:

> Whoever I associate with,
> May I think of myself
>   as though I were the lowest among all
> And respectfully hold others to be supreme
> From the very depths of my heart.

We must cultivate awareness to be with our feelings, not stuck in them, so we don't get bogged down in the patterns of depression, anxiety, or self-hatred. You are a kind, beautiful, wonderful person with so much potential, and you can't have genuine love for others if you can't have love for yourself. So please try to take that meaning into your heart.

In the same way, remember that people who behave and speak in a cruel or manipulative or unskillful way are only doing that because of their delusion, their insecurities and fears. They need compassion more than most. Even when we meet someone who comes across as really annoying or nasty, we can try to slow down the judging mind and check, before we notice their faults, what are their qualities? If that is really hard, then we can remember that although their karma is very strong in this life, in a previous life they could have been our kind mother or brother who underwent so many hardships for us out of devotional love and caring.

In terms of rebirth, we have a body and we have awareness. The body we can touch; we know about its birth and death; it changes. Awareness we can't touch and describe, but it has a continuum. There is no beginning to awareness, so from beginningless time, unendingly, every sentient being has at one time been our tremendously kind mother. But due to the changes from rebirth, we see some as enemies, some as indifferent, but actually, everyone is our mother. That is why we must hold them all dear from the depths of our hearts.

So right now, think about this: "Every sentient being is my beloved mother. Hey, Mom, you know I love you. You have done so much for me. I will never be able to repay your kindness. I can't bear to think of you unhappy or lonely or scared or in pain. I won't stop until you are completely free from all suffering."

Let's think like that, not just as a nice idea but with passion from the depths of our hearts until we totally reverse our way of thinking, from ourselves as the most important and others as "Well, only if I have the time," to our mothers as most important and ourselves as "Oh, you again? Well, only if I have the time."

May I Inquire into My Own Mind

Now, we might think that some people are genuinely superior but that some are really lower than us: the kind of guys who make snide remarks; smart alecks who put us down or patronize us; bullies; people who use others or who feel justified to impose their selfish will over us. You know what I'm talking about. How do we avoid that? Because we all know guys like that, right? Well, that's what this third verse is about:

> In all activities,
>   may I inquire into my own mind,

And as soon as an afflictive emotion arises,
Endangering both myself and others,
May I firmly face and repel it.

This means that we must always examine our minds in our daily life—not just through formal meditation, but even when we're eating, sitting, walking the dog, spending time with our friends, and so on. Then, as soon as any form of attachment, anger, jealousy, or any disturbing force arises, challenge it, because these afflictive emotions cause nothing but chaos—not just in this life, but in terms of lower rebirth in the future too. No outer enemy can do that, but the inner afflictions can.

There is no worse enemy than our own afflictive emotions and nothing in this world more dangerous.

Afflictive emotions are the source of all our pain and suffering, yet we've been hanging out with them for so long that even when we identify them as the cause of suffering, they can be like an addiction that's very hard to give up.

Those who haven't had the fortune of meeting with the precious teachings have no real idea that the afflictive emotions are the cause of suffering. They even think people who fight with anger can be heroes when, from our point of view, they have already been defeated, because afflictive emotions are the cause of our misery. We must all realize that the cause of suffering is getting caught up in the afflictive emotions.

For most of us, afflictive emotions are easy to stimulate. Words alone can arouse anger. But the very first step to changing this is to realize that the real enemy is within.

Then we have to confront the affliction, such as anger, when it arises. Normally, when anger arises, we think in such a way that more anger comes. We get so caught up in it that sooner or later we can end up hurting others. So instead, when anger arises, we repel it, knowing that nothing but stress will be its fruit.

Just think—the moment anger arises in the heart, peace disappears. It's like on my one free afternoon of the week in India, just getting to the real climax in a nail-biting thriller, then just at that moment, the inevitable power outage comes and spoils everything.

Anger affects our appetite and our sleep; it feeds anxiety and pain and makes us more stressed out. Empathy, however, will make us stronger, calmer, emotionally balanced, happy, and at ease in our life. So we must overcome afflictive emotions and instead develop positive states of mind. Indulging in anger leads to stress; therefore, we counteract it with loving-kindness and compassion.

When anger arises, instead of automatically going along with it, we can examine it: Where does it come from? Where does it abide? Where does it pass? We will see that such thoughts are unabiding; they are adventitious stains in the mind, but not of the mind's true nature. We can overcome the darkness of anger through the light of wisdom. With this wisdom of discernment, we can eliminate the addiction of self-cherishing.

May I Cherish the Bad

Even if we have to deal with really negative people, we should think that we have discovered a great opportunity, not just to curb our reactivity, like anger, but also to practice responsiveness by being patient and empathetic. Negative people are more worthy of our empathy because when we empathize with them, we see that toxic ignorance and indulgence in afflictive emotions are the cause of their behavior; therefore, we cherish them, as is stated in this fourth verse:

> May I cherish beings of bad nature,
> Those oppressed by the experience
>   of forceful misdeeds and suffering,
> As if I had found a treasury of precious jewels
> Very difficult to find.

It's like if a beggar found treasure, he couldn't give it up, so let's think that we have found unbelievable treasure in the form of sentient beings and resolve that we will save them. Without others, we can't practice Buddhism properly. Without them, we cannot achieve the awakening of bodhi. We need to have open hearts for those who aggravate us in order to develop patience, without which we will never cultivate the merit to become a supreme savior. If we ignore them, hurt them, steal from them, hate them, or lead them astray, it will be like a poor person finding a diamond and just throwing it away. So let's treasure others without any artifice or inhibition, and foster those feelings every day.

May I Offer Them Victory

The actual exchange practice of mind training has two aspects: offering victory in words and exchanging the victory in meaning. The first, giving victory in words, relates to unpleasant verbal exchanges such as taking the blame oneself in an argument. This exchange is mentioned in the fifth verse:

> When others, out of envy, treat me badly
> With abuse, scorn, and the like,
> May I voluntarily join the losing side
> And offer victory to them.

Up until now, we've tried always to prove ourselves to be faultless and innocent, and we've always blamed others. But no matter what the abuse or slander or name-calling aimed at us, we accept it and offer the victory to the other side.

Quite some time ago, when I was small, I had a friend, and I always used to blame him for everything. Like when I broke stuff or took sweets without permission, I always pointed my finger at him, so he would get scolded instead of me. Yeah, I know I was very naughty at that time! So one day, we went to one of my teachers, a very great lama. We were just playing one day and that time he really did break something; it was a big, old-fashioned, wooden back scratcher. It was on the lama's table, so it had to be his. My friend was so scared and nervous; he didn't know what to do. I felt so bad for him, and he was crying, so I had to save his skin back then. I told him, "Don't worry, I will tell them that I did it." He hesitated at first, but then said, "Don't say that, I will admit that I did it," so we had a big argument. I said it was me, but he tried to save me, saying that he did it and started crying. Then someone told us, "Ah, don't worry, it's nothing! It doesn't even belong to the lama and we were going to throw it out anyway." All that time we were arguing for nothing.

There are examples of this among the great Buddhist masters in the past, like one who was accused of stealing and even though he didn't do it, he accepted the blame as part of his practice. We should aspire to be as unconditionally loving as that.

May I See Them as a Spiritual Friend

This is one thing in theory, but it's not so easy in practice. The sixth verse explains the practical application of this attitude with someone who directly affects us:

> When one whom I have benefited
> And in whom I have placed great hopes
> Treats me very badly, may I see that kind of person
> As a sacred spiritual friend.

Haven't we all gone through some dynamic with someone close to us that leaves us feeling a weight on our shoulders, hurt, let down, stuck, helpless? Like when something happens and it shatters our peace and well-being; an unpleasant incident or exchange of words that might not be so upsetting with someone we're not so close to, but with someone we love and trust, it becomes something really visceral.

Normally, when we help someone, we expect reciprocity. If we're nice to others, we expect them to be nice to us. So even though I helped someone, if they act badly toward me, I might feel justified in getting angry, but as we've already examined, anger only causes suffering. If we're always mindful of this, these people are the best teachers to give us the chance to actually implement patience, love, and compassion.

This verse explains that even those who mistreat us in the most challenging way—that is, they hurt us and let us down all the more because we have formed trust and affection with them—are not to be viewed as our enemies but rather as our precious teachers. Those who hurt and mistreat us are the ones we must help and benefit especially, instead of taking revenge out of heedless resentment.

Before, when I was staying in my grandparents' place, I knew a boy who would come to play with me. He always made me do stuff for him, such as bring him sweets and games to play—my toys—and if I didn't, he said he wouldn't play with me, which would make me kind of lonely. I admit that I resented him ordering me around so much, but it was the only way to have company. I knew he was very poor, and one day I teased him about it, so he was very sad and cried. Then I felt so bad and wanted to help him, so I gave him my favorite—and his favorite—Power Ranger toy. That really cheered him up, but it was a huge sacrifice for me at that time. So like that, we must help and be kind to the persons who mistreat or hurt us instead of taking revenge. Bullies only do what they do out of fear, loneliness, and insecurity, so we can never stop bullying through countermeasures alone. Bullies need our warmth and help to break out of their prisons of fear.

May I Offer Happiness and Take Others' Suffering upon Myself

Whether one is a Buddhist practitioner or not, no matter what, we all want to be free from suffering; we're all longing to be blissful. Everyone's trying to achieve that in their life in their own way, but due to misknowing, the majority of us, despite what we really want, just compound the causes of suffering and throw away the causes of bliss. That is why our world is a world of massive suffering and it's only getting worse. We are suffering due to misknowing.

What I mean is that instead of seeing the true nature of mind, we cling to a false notion of identity without real reasons. If we examine it carefully, we can't find anything to really call my "self." If there is a self, it has to be the name, the body, or the mind.

The name? Of course not—any name could be given at any time. My name is not "me."

The body? No, that's many things together. Examine it from head to toe; all the flesh, bones, and so forth. Take any one component separately and that can't be your "self," so how could the body be "me"?

The mind is changing moment to moment. How could something in constant flux be your "self"? Even in ordinary usage, when we say, "This is my house," this belongs to me but is not me, so when we say, "my body," it belongs to me but is not me, and when we say, "my mind," it belongs to me, but who is this great owner? I have never found him.

We have this strongly built-up habit of self-clinging without any logic behind it. So like mistaking a rope for a snake, we can't be free from fear and anxiety with this misknowing. As long as we cling to a false notion of self, we can't be free from the fears and anxieties of samsara. As soon as we realize selflessness, we are free from fear forever, just like when we realize the snake is really a rope and our fear disappears. The root of this fear and pain is self-clinging.

The most powerful practice to combat and overcome this strong habit is giving and receiving, known in Tibetan as *tonglen*—the exchange practice of giving and taking. We then overcome self-cherishing and attain the bliss that never ceases. If we had done this practice long ago, we would not be full of stress now. The difference between the buddhas and ordinary people like us is that buddhas have given up self-cherishing and so achieve their own welfare and the welfare of others, whereas we ordinary people harbor self-cherishing and tend to care more about ourselves and just a small unit of close ones, and so we experience more and more stress.

Such practice is a challenge, but we must train our minds to start in the right direction. Even just to make a start in this practice is of unbelievable benefit.

Someone who was the most precious person, a person who has been so kind to you, thought about you, and taken care of you—even if their life was in danger, you would sacrifice yourself for that person without hesitation. You wouldn't want that person to get hurt or feel lonely or suffer. You would want to make that person's suffering go away, to exchange their suffering for your own joy. Just like that, we should imagine that that person is all sentient beings. And we don't just imagine this—all of them really are our loved ones, so we should think of exchanging all sentient beings' suffering with our joy as much as possible:

> In short, may I offer all my mothers
> All hope and happiness, directly and indirectly,
> And secretly take upon myself
> All their harm and suffering.

Now, to do the tonglen practice, I find it helpful to start with myself. For that, just start by relaxing the mind in a comfortable meditation posture and place attention on the breathing. Follow the flow of breathing through the body, and after some time you notice areas that don't feel so good—maybe some pain, tension, coldness, and so forth. Then meditate that as you breathe in, all of those difficult feelings take the form of black smoke or an oil slick and dissolve in the heart. Then, as you breathe out, beautiful light or nectar permeates the whole body, filling it with bliss and healing. In that way, we are not trying to push our pain away or just blindly ignore it, nor are we painstakingly trying to psychoanalyze it, which is endless. We're simply giving loving-kindness to ourselves by being with and attuning to the subtler aspects of our experience and filtering out the impurities, instead of being stuck in and overwhelmed by emotive turbulence.

Then, from that basis, we move on to visualize in front of ourselves our most cherished loved one. This can be your kind mother or anyone you feel an instant concern and deep affection for, like a body reflex, the moment you think of that person. Think that they are just like you in that they want to be happy and avoid pain, and you would do whatever it takes to place them in bliss and take them away from all misery. In a relaxed way, imagine that as you breathe in, you suck all their pain away like a vacuum cleaner into your left nostril, so that all their pain and causes of pain are pulled out of their right nostril by your power in the form of a dark cloud, black smoke, or an oil slick, and it comes down to your heart, where it melts into emptiness. As you breathe out, all your happiness and causes of happiness are bestowed upon them in the form of brilliant light, a rainbow, or nectar, which leaves your right nostril, goes into their left nostril, and floods their whole body, placing them in the stage of a buddha. So in that way, you take on all their sicknesses, negative karma, and obscurations, and you give away all your well-being, virtues, and qualities.

Don't worry, this won't make us sick or give us their problems, nor are we throwing our virtues and qualities in the garbage. But this wishing does have power for bringing healing to others and deepening our empathy.

We then continue with this breathing process but dissolve the visualization into emptiness and take it to the next level by now imagining someone we are usually indifferent to. Who read the news this morning on TV? Who served you your meal in the café? Who walked past you on your way to work yesterday? In other words, people who don't really affect us so much, either good or bad. Think that they were your dear loved one in a previous life and do exactly the same meditation of the exchange with the breathing.

Then, we go even deeper. We visualize those who we could call enemies—not necessarily a major enemy, but someone who causes you anger or annoyance, someone who has been unkind, cruel, or hurtful to you or your loved ones. We already reflected that it is vital that we direct empathy to them rather than thoughts of hatred or vengeance. So thinking that the word *enemy* has no meaning in your life anymore, arouse the same love and compassion with the same breathing meditation of the exchange. This may be hard to do, but I really can't put into words how amazingly powerful this tonglen meditation can be. We just have to practice.

In the text, you'll see that it says, I "secretly" do this meditation. That's because this teaching on the exchange wasn't put in general Buddhist texts for regular practitioners; it was kept restricted only for the most advanced Mahayana meditators who have the determination, courage, and universal love to do it seriously. It's for superhero bodhisattvas!

Now, when it says to "take upon myself all their harm and suffering," it isn't enough just to do a visualization exercise; we have to think about that deeply. If someone who gets on your nerves is shouting in your face, it's unlikely that you will think first and foremost of that person's suffering, but even then, for superhero bodhisattvas, we have to remember and take on their suffering in our hearts. At the very least, we need to have the aspiration to develop such skill. This is something to do quietly, privately; it's like we are keeping our superhero identity a secret. We do this in our everyday life, so we don't need to put on a cape and cowl to show off. Otherwise, we might practice contrary to what we're trying to achieve and build up expectations that we later feel we can't live up to. So it's something to do with care.

May I Understand That All Phenomena Are Illusions

As the last verse explains, for this practice to be authentic, we have to keep it uncontaminated with interfering concepts that can creep into our minds—the desire to be praised by others or to have it make us immediately cheerful and so on:

> May I keep all these practices free from conflation
> With the stains of the eight worldly concepts and,
> By understanding that all phenomena are illusions,
> Be released from the bondage of clinging.

The essence of the last verse is about the ultimate bodhichitta, which has to be free from all concepts and limiting extremes and then, as it says, all of these practices, including the cultivation of the relative bodhichitta that we have contemplated in the preceding seven verses.

From my experience, I think it's very useful to explore the two bodhichittas in more depth by studying *Entering the Bodhisattva's Way of Life*.

Nourishing the Seed of a Buddha

We have all got a bit too used to the way of thinking that is under the sway of the eight worldly concepts, but if we practice these teachings, we can give up that bad habit. Every one of us is endowed with what is known as the seed of a buddha—the innate buddha nature, which is the essence of our minds, like the sun that is always present behind the clouds. Due to that, we can also erase attachment to all the eight worldly concepts and their related defilements from our inner hard drive, and then the sun of our awakened mind will shine forth.

The seed of any crop, to make it grow, needs fertile soil, water, sunlight, and so forth. In the same way, we need certain conditions to ripen the mind, to evolve the heart to full maturity. What are those conditions that we need?

The first condition is refuge. Having recognized the qualities of the Triple Gem, which we can't find anywhere else, we go for refuge until we attain completely perfect awakening: to the Buddha as our guide on the path, to the Dharma as the path itself, and to the Sangha as our companions to support us on the path. This is the awakening condition, in that it awakens the seed within us.

To enrich or nourish the seed, we need the conditions of love and compassion. If we nurture these three conditions, then our harvest will definitely grow without any impairment.

Now here is one important thing. I met a monk in a temple in India; we were having a Dharma discussion, and I soon realized that he was very skilled in memorizing rituals and chants. Then I happened to ask him about a particular important prayer we do, "Do you find *The Majestic Aspiration of Aryabhadra* helpful to develop your understanding of the bodhisattva practice?" He confessed to me, "Rinpoche, although I have memorized many prayers, I've no idea what they mean." Now, that's a real shame. I also have some Western Buddhist friends who talk to me, and some of them told me that at first they were really diligent and inspired, but after some time the novelty wore off and they became a bit lax or something. That's a lack of patience, I think. So whether in the East or West, it's very important to keep it simple, to keep it real. If we don't think about the meaning—or even if we do but we neglect to think deeply and continually so we just relate to Dharma on a superficial level—then our enthusiasm can deteriorate.

If we take the meaning of those three things—refuge, love, and compassion—into our hearts truly and deeply and often, and if we then care for others, wanting to protect them and help them, then the benefits from our practice for ourselves will all come naturally. This will be our continual source of self-encouragement and determination.

When I talk about cherishing others deeply, this is not just what we need to do on a meditation cushion surrounded by nice Dharma friends and famous teachers, because we could sit on a cushion all day saying, "I'm thinking of others" but never really do anything to help them. Although meditation is good and important, we must take our practice off the cushion and into the world, as really cherishing others is how bodhichitta arises. This has to be vast and universal, not limited in any way by bias or discrimination. On the basis of that, the strong aspiration, and the vows of restraint, such as refraining from the ten unvirtuous deeds and so forth, we then take the commitment to engage bodhichitta, which the eight verses are really about.

Then there are three trainings we observe.

Refraining from Unvirtuous Deeds

The first of the three trainings is refraining from unvirtuous deeds. In this context, this means, first, refraining from anger by cherishing all beings; second, exchanging the blame; third, resolving not to react in anger; and fourth, cherishing others as more important than oneself.

Remember, as Shantideva said, we need sentient beings as much as we need the Buddha. Of course, the Buddha is so important and worthy of homage, but we need sentient beings in order to develop bodhichitta and practice what the Buddha told us to do. So we need to implement this advice by respecting sentient beings as much as the Buddha. None of us is in a position to judge others' minds, only our own, so we should sharpen our attention to what our minds are doing in the here and now and not worry about what may or may not be going on in the consciousness of anyone else. We need to develop constant mindfulness and discernment for this, which will naturally decrease the afflictive emotions of anger and clinging so we are able to stop them before they manage to take hold in the mind.

Now, some Buddhist practitioners feel the need to avoid people and other distractions, like monks preferring to hide away in jungle groves and mountain caves and places like that so that they can develop deep meditation to escape from samsara. Mahayana practitioners can certainly develop their practice by doing retreats, and that's very good, but we actually don't need to deepen our practice that way. That is why these teachings are really helpful for us in the modern world with busy lives, families, work, and so forth, because we use these teachings to utilize challenging circumstances to develop the transcendent perfections, such as patience. Also, difficult people need the bodhisattvas' help more than most, because ordinary people will probably shun them. So we must not be afraid of challenging circumstances and difficult people, but rather welcome them with open arms, as this is how our Dharma practice will really come to life. It can even be better for our practice.

Benefiting All Beings

The second training is to benefit all beings. What we have to avoid is retaliating with harm, whether it is verbal or physical, so we respond rather than react. Then what we have to do to benefit sentient beings relates to the three forms of giving: giving material gifts, giving fearlessness, and giving the Dharma. What augments this is seeing everyone, especially those who cause us problems, as spiritual guides.

All of this—practicing giving and taking the blame instead of insisting on always being right—goes against the grain of what we are accustomed to doing in protecting our sense of self. In terms of the bodhisattva's way of life, that is really a good thing, because it means we are actually breaking the chains of attachment, of self-clinging.

Amassing Virtue

Amassing virtuous deeds is inseparable from the accumulation of wisdom, the essence of the eighth verse. The accumulation of wisdom actually relates directly to amassing virtuous deeds, because we need both together, like a bird needs two wings to fly. Our present wisdom is not enough because we need nonconceptual wisdom beyond the eight worldly concerns. The conceptual mind operates in dualistic terms that mistakenly posit me and mine, this and that, so the worldly concepts—gain and loss, happiness and unhappiness, praise and blame, fame and infamy—come into force. In conceptual terms, we ourselves are the bodhisattvas, all other sentient beings are the objects, and the action is the precepts of training. We do need to take this view, of course, but ultimately, we need the absolute bodhichitta beyond relative concepts to understand the way things truly are.

If we cling to or identify ourselves as the subject, the giver, and sentient beings as the object, then we are tied to the three worlds of samsara (desire, subtle form, and formlessness). So the eighth verse is presented to transcend that. When we separate these things—subject, object, and action—clinging arises. Then the eight worldly concepts arise.

We all want to have happiness, to avoid suffering, to be complimented, and so forth, but the real practitioner must be beyond the illusions of criticism, fame, and so on. We must remember that what appears as me and mine and so on is like a dream, and maintain the meditation of appearances as illusory, so that we learn to trust in awareness, like waking up fresh and alert from a dream, ready to greet whatever appears with the mind that is knowing and loving.

In a way, this collects virtuous deeds, which we need in order to generate the wisdom that realizes voidness. When we see all phenomena as illusory, like a dream, the result is that eventually we will be free—truly and forever free—from the three worlds of samsara. We will attain all the qualities of a buddha. Then, forever and always, we will be free from bondage, from being tied up in negativities and obscurations, which will be nothing but a distant memory. We will never react; karma will be transcended, and instead we will respond to the suffering of all mother sentient beings out of our uncontrived, non-referential compassion with the transcendental activities of boundless emanations. Actually, as I said, I'm still a beginner myself, but if you get any ideas or inspiration from this Dharma sharing, I hope it will bring benefit to your life.

Let us make a dedication that through whatever merit has arisen from studying, contemplating, and cultivating these precious mind-training teachings, we will attain the stage of a buddha very quickly for the welfare of all mother sentient beings.

7

As Fearless as Tara

As the Buddha himself said in the *Sutra Requested by Viryadatta*:

> If the merit of bodhichitta were to take physical form, even the whole of space itself could not contain it.

In today's materialistic world, which has so many ups and downs and not so many people turning their minds to virtue, let alone to ideas of transcendence, we must feel a real sense of joy and enthusiasm to be able to learn and think about and practice the dispensation of the Buddha, which leads not just to happiness in this life but also to the ultimate bliss of liberation and enlightenment. Especially, we are learning and contemplating and cultivating bodhichitta, the mind that aspires to the stage of a buddha for the sake of all wandering beings, our mothers. Really taking those words of the Buddha to heart, we can feel great inspiration, enthusiasm and momentum to consider the meaning of the teachings deeply in our minds and to resolve to practice properly in order to actualize their meaning. As the Buddha also said in the *Sutra of the Wise and the Foolish*:

Don't disregard small virtues, thinking that they don't have much benefit, because even tiny drops of water will eventually fill a big pot.

So even though we might think this is like any other teaching, or we could think, "Yeah, yeah, I've read loads of profound teachings; this isn't so important really," actually we must recollect the four foundations—the preciousness of a human life, impermanence, the law of cause and effect, and the suffering of unenlightened existence—as well as refuge, and the proper motivation before studying any teaching, any time, by any authentic teacher, otherwise it would be a real waste.

Actually, when I was studying in monasteries in India, it could be easy to just get used to it and see the classes as slightly boring lectures, like when you're at high school and you want to go hang out with your buddies at the mall or go skateboarding or something instead. However, I tried to remember these things every time I had class, so my mind would feel fresh and a sort of a grounded enthusiasm, something warm and uplifted, each time I received teachings. Then, because I feel happy and relaxed and motivated, I notice that my mind stays quite clear and I can absorb and understand the teachings I receive much better than when I'm tired and dull. So try to shift into that gear, feel that warm, fresh feeling, and recollect what a precious opportunity we have.

In the *Gandhavyuha Sutra*, there's one passage by the Buddha that I read quite some time ago, and as soon as I read it, I found it very beautiful, very helpful. So I memorized it, and I say it mentally to myself before I receive any Dharma teaching:

> Children of the family, give rise to the thought
> "I am the patient who is unwell";
> Give rise to the thought
> "The Dharma is the medicine";

Give rise to the thought
"The virtuous guide is the expert doctor";
And give rise to the thought
"Diligent practice is the way to be really cured."

Here, the Buddha calls us "children of the family" because we are of the Mahayana family. When we generate the aspiration to attain the stage of a buddha for the welfare of all our kind mothers of former lives, nothing could please the buddhas more; not just gods but the great bodhisattvas and buddhas rejoice when we generate bodhichitta and, from that moment on, they think of us as their beloved children and bestow their blessings and protection. Shantideva said in *Entering the Bodhisattva's Way of Life*:

Now my life is fruitful.
Human existence is well obtained.
Today I have been born in the family of buddhas;
I have become a son of the Buddha.

Now, in whatever situation,
I will only undertake actions that accord with the
    family;
Never shall I bring taint
To this undefiled venerable family.

Followers of the southern school of Theravada Buddhism actually have to have razor-sharp mindfulness at all times, so they aspire to receive teachings with a proper motivation according to their own scope, and we can say that for *any* successful learning process, *any* kind of student also needs a strong motivation. So how much more so for those who have the highest scope, the motivation of the northern school of Mahayana Buddhism?

The Three Types of Practitioner

To give some elucidation on this, the great Bengali scholar Atisha, who spent many years in Tibet teaching Mahayana Buddhism and who made a prophecy about the founding of Sakya monastery there, explained in his classic treatise *The Lamp for the Path to Awakening* that there are three types of people or practitioners.

The first are the inferior persons who realize that this life is not permanent, that one day we all have to leave this world. We have this body and mind, and when we leave this world, the body will be disposed of in one way or another. The mind, however, is not something visible or tangible, so it can't be disposed of as we dispose of the body, nor does it just disappear. The continuity of consciousness, or, rather, its karmic energy, goes on. When we leave this world, nothing follows us. All our relatives, friends, possessions, and this body that we hold so dear—we have to leave everything behind. But our karma—all our positive and negative actions, the virtuous and unvirtuous deeds that we have done—will follow us, just like our shadow follows us wherever we go. The unvirtuous deeds that we have committed will cause us to experience lower realms of existence where we will have to experience very severe suffering. The virtuous deeds that we have done while we're here will cause us to continuously be born in the higher realms. So those who are afraid to be reborn in the lower realms and wish to be reborn continuously in the higher realms and who have this as their motivation—Atisha referred to such persons as the inferior practitioners. Although their goal is a positive one, it is still within the cycle of compulsive existence.

However, even with that scope, I think at least two of the four foundations, which we all need to recollect over and over and contemplate very deeply, apply here. So, number one, even at this stage, we're recognizing the preciousness of a human rebirth in which we can practice some kind of spirituality, we can gather merit and so on, otherwise we wouldn't be talking about any kind of practitioner at all; we'd have to resign ourselves to mindless hedonism or something. So we're incredibly fortunate to have the precious human life with all its advantages and opportunities, and must not waste this opportunity. Then number two, we're recognizing the law of karma, and so we live our lives accordingly.

Then there are those who realize that it's not only in the lower realms that we have to experience very severe suffering, but even the higher realms are unsatisfactory. If we examine it carefully, the happiness of the higher realms, such as a celestial existence where every wish is granted, is not real happiness; it is only happiness in appearance. In reality, even the higher realms are suffering, because as captivating as they might be, they can't last forever and they're actually too captivating, so it's like a dead end for Dharma practice. At that level, we also include the other two of the four foundations: impermanence—the fact that all conditioned phenomena are transitory—and the faults and unsatisfactory nature of samsara, of suffering. One who wishes to be totally free from the whole cycle of compulsive existence and seeks nirvana, permanent peace, is what Atisha called a mediocre practitioner. Although it is a very great thing—the attainment being that all the causes of one's own suffering cease—it's not the final goal, because one has not perfected one's full potential. Although in the mediocre attainment one does not have afflictive obscurations, one still has the cognitive obscurations to accomplishing complete omniscience.

Then, having gained a tangible feeling in our hearts about the four foundations—to make the most of this precious human life, then understand impermanence, karma, and the suffering of samsara—we can look at the goal of a "child of the family," or what Atisha referred to as the superior practitioner. So we accept the premise of rebirth, that from beginningless time until now, we are all caught up in the cycle of compulsive existence. That means that one way or another every sentient being is related to us; every sentient being has given us so much love and care and so much benefit, just like our dear relatives and friends in this present life have given us. To forget about them and just seek peace for ourselves alone is just unthinkable for a child of the family. I don't think it's possible to survive without depending on anybody else. We have been brought up in this present life through the immense help and kindness of others. For example, our present life is thanks to our parents. Our parents took care of us when we were newborns and incapable of doing anything; they have brought us up, and so have our friends, our teachers, and so on. Having been cared for in this way, we have managed to become a capable human being. Then even as an adult, we still have to depend on love and care and help from others, otherwise what kind of life would that be? And as we get older, we have to depend even more on the kindness of others. So in this very life, our entire life is thanks to the help and kindness given by others. How can we not care for the welfare of other sentient beings?

For the Sake of All Sentient Beings

Although everyone wants to be blissful, the vast majority, due to misknowing or ignorance, create more and more causes for suffering, and experience more and more suffering. We need to have deep, heartfelt compassion for those who are experiencing suffering, and this is the root, the very first seed, of becoming a buddha.

Our present conceptual form of compassion is limited and insufficient, because we actually need to rescue *all* sentient beings from suffering and place them on the path of happiness. We ourselves, although we may have great feelings, are limited; we do not have complete wisdom, compassion, and ability, so we can't really save sentient beings from samsara like that. Even the most powerful worldly deities cannot free sentient beings from the suffering of samsara. Not only the worldly deities but even those who have attained static nirvana cannot rescue all sentient beings. The only one who can really save all sentient beings is a buddha who possesses omniscient wisdom, boundless compassion, and inconceivable abilities. So our goal is to accomplish such a state, the state of a buddha, for the sake of the limitless sentient beings.

With that goal in mind, we go for refuge. The mediocre practitioners go for refuge out of a kind of fear of the suffering in samsara, as we have explored. But the superior practitioners aren't just scared of suffering themselves; they are actually terrified that their beloved mothers have to undergo so much pain. They can't bear it. So they see the immense qualities of the guru and Triple Gem, and their hearts are relieved. They then automatically aspire to attain such qualities themselves and, having explored the teachings, they have the courage and conviction that this is what they will do. With the altruistic attitude that they must do this for the sake of all their beloved mothers, they go for refuge. So with the four foundations firm in our continuum and with the three types of faith, they go for refuge for the welfare of all sentient beings equal to the bounds of space.

Just as space has no limits, sentient beings also have no limits. For the limitless sentient beings, we must attain the full, perfect bodhi. In every practice we do as practitioners of the causal Mahayana, the vehicle of the transcendent perfections, as well as the resultant Mahayana, which is the Vajrayana, our final goal is bodhi. Whether we're receiving initiations, studying teachings, or doing our practice diligently with joyful vigor, our ultimate goal is to attain the ultimate bodhi, the state of a buddha.

Who Is Tara?

I should say something about why we consider the meditations and recitations of Tara so very important in our tradition and why Tibetan Buddhists rely on her so much. It is said that Tara was born from the compassionate tears of Avalokiteshvara, the great bodhisattva of compassion, and so she carries out the loving activities of the buddhas. Why is that?

Well, the historical Buddha Shakyamuni, as we know, was a kind of prince who displayed his renunciation, turned the wheel of Dharma three times, and spent about forty years giving innumerable teachings for the sake of rescuing all wandering beings from samsara. He is our teacher, our guide; he is like the main exemplar of enlightenment for our time. In ordinary terms, he was born with the name Siddhartha Gautama, but after he attained complete bodhi, he didn't want to be known by his birth name; he referred to himself as the Buddha, and also the Tathagata, the Sugata, and so on. The reason is that he had attained the state of realization and cessation beyond all description, beyond all extremes and limits, beyond all karma, which these names remind us of. Actually, we can say that the Buddha is beyond the ideas of male and female as we ordinarily think of them. This can help us understand why in the Vajrayana teachings in particular, the Buddha appears in so many different forms: male and female, male and female together, peaceful, passionate, wrathful, and so on—because of how they are helpful to our minds.

We are all the same in that we all want to be blissful and free and to go beyond stress, stuckness, and confusion; we are all endowed with the seed of buddha nature, and definitely we are all equal in deserving the same rights as equal members of humanity. However, it is fair to say that we all have our own unique DNA; we all have slightly different dispositions, characteristics, habits, and so on. That's why there's such a variety of meditational deities in the Vajrayana, so we can have a karmic connection to whichever meditational deity will suit us best, and then the resulting attainments will come much more expediently through that practice. The deities in Vajrayana—the transcendental deities, that is, not worldly deities but tutelary deities—we call yidams in Tibetan, are beyond the constraints of karma; they are not separate, in fact, from the body, speech, mind, qualities, and activities of the Buddha.

In the case of Tara, there's some special significance. She is known as the one who helps us accomplish all our activities and who liberates us from fear; she rescues us from the eight great fears in particular. Now, ordinary people like me—and we can see this in young children perhaps more easily—when we're scared, when we're really in the grip of fear, the most natural response is to want our mom, to call out to our mother, to want her tender embrace to comfort us and shield us from that fear. It's something so, so amazing that Tara made the vow that she will always appear in female form to give her tender embrace, to comfort us like that and liberate us from terror, until samsara is ended for everyone. This actually relates to our natural instincts. We should really remember that and take it to heart.

Tara's Protection

Now, we can think, "OK, but, hey, I'm not a little kid anymore. I've got to stand on my own two feet, be independent, confident, and look after myself." That's OK. I'm not suggesting that Tara is only for weak people, for sissies, or something like that. How come so many seemingly big brave guys in Buddhist countries in Asia have relied so much on the practice of Tara? That's worth some serious reflection.

Actually, no matter how tough we think we are or would like to be, the Buddha had something to say about that. He compared the human condition to being like a cow with her skin flayed in the middle of a crossroads in the Indian summer. If you've ever been to India, you might be able to relate to that. It's a very graphic description, isn't it? He actually said that to be conscious was an experience of vulnerability. Let's think about that, because the experience of sense consciousness is not a personal thing that we can just decide to be resilient about. We're not really as much in control as we pretend to be. To be conscious through the senses, which we all are, is a kind of impingement. There's such a variety of sense objects that consciousness receives through the door of the eyes, the ears, the nose, the tongue, the body, and the thinking mind too. We need sleep just to let our brains and nervous systems have a time-out from that contact, because in the course of just one day, we'll experience so many things. Some we want and find pleasurable, and we get frustrated when we can't have them; some we don't want and find disturbing, and we stress out when we have to endure them. It goes on and on and on like that, and we call that cycle the beginningless cycle of samsara, the cycle of compulsive existence that never brings any ultimate satisfaction.

How Fear Operates

In his unique exposition of dependent origination, that everything, including mental states, comes into being from a variety of causes and conditions and is impermanent, the Buddha explained how this cycle keeps going on, just like we see in traditional Buddhist paintings of the wheel of life. He explained that, due to the blindness of misknowing, the crafting of volitional formatives occurs, then through the mischievous monkey of consciousness, the duality is contrived of labels and separate forms, which operates through the windows of the six senses, the basis of contact, which is the target for Cupid's arrow of feelings, for which we get the thirst of craving and so forth, the end result being the vicious cycle of birth, death, and dissatisfaction.

Notice that so long as we have not overcome misknowing—which means as long as we have not fully accumulated merit and wisdom, and so have not overcome the afflictive and cognitive obscurations—we're still programmed to operate in terms of duality. Now, that's a very good thing, because it means that when we target that root of misknowing through the realization of voidness beyond the four limiting extremes—when we have awakened self-awareness of the way it is in final reality—then the whole vicious cycle stops. We can experience cessation. That's the ceasing of all karma, of all afflictions, of all anxiety, doubt, and fear.

What this points to is that it's not enough to simply try to block out or numb the human experience of consciousness to suppress our fears. That's just not going to last in the long term; it won't liberate us. What I mean is that people without any sort of spiritual training might try blocking or numbing their experience with something like alcohol or drugs, which, of course, is a mistaken path. But even spiritual people can try to go on some kind of meditation trip all the time, trying to dismiss everything as trivial and distracting, and then always want to be in a state of sensory deprivation by going into their meditation trance. If we look at a statue of the Buddha, the Buddha has his eyes slightly open; he's very peaceful, but he's not trying to shut out the world. He recognized that in the basic conditions of human experience—of birth, aging, sickness, death, loss, grief, loneliness; feeling misunderstood; not feeling heard; feeling unfulfilled; feeling stressed, scared, and worried—in these things, we are all the same; we are all vulnerable through consciousness so long as we haven't fully awakened to truth. But all of those experiences and feelings are impermanent, they all have causes and conditions, and they all cease when the ultimate nondual wisdom has been actualized.

We must also remember that fear isn't always *about* something. Sometimes I feel this kind of contraction, this kind of heat in my solar plexus that I associate with a kind of fear, but it doesn't have to have a special story line attached to it. I often just go to that feeling without any particular goal to push it away or work it out, and then I can relax into its fading away. If I just ignore it or get too complicated with it, I notice it can actually get worse.

How to Be Fearless

Appearances to the mind through the senses arise and cease, and feelings also arise and cease. Through Dharma practice, we can gain insight into that process in our own minds while still on the path to lessen a lot of our coarse emotive reactivity, which enables us to develop virtue and merit and to prevent degrading misdeeds and faults. Calm-abiding meditation and special insight meditation are the key means for that process, and we need mindfulness in all activities, too, in order to have an integrated approach. The real goal we must keep in mind is to evolve to our fullest potential, to ripen the seed of buddha nature within us to full fruit in order to help everyone overcome the vicious cycle of samsara by accumulating merit and wisdom.

We need this because we're not looking to a god or goddess outside ourselves to intervene every time we feel frightened or upset. We need to recognize the root of our fears, which is misknowing. Only we can do that ourselves. All the buddhas' and bodhisattvas' loving activity comes together in the form of Tara to support us in that endeavor, which is really possible because her blessings can help us tap into and affirm our own buddha nature, acting as a condition to ripen the results of previously accumulated virtues that we have done, which might not otherwise have ripened yet. Not only does she liberate us from ordinary fears, she brings us to the ultimate state of fearlessness, which is the supreme attainment.

The Eight Great Fears

There are some variations that I have seen in my studies, but mainly there are eight great fears that we can talk about that Tara protects us from.

First, she rescues us from water. In ordinary terms, that means floods and drowning. There have actually been cases where people were swept away in a river, then called out to Tara and survived. In higher terms, though, it means that she liberates us from being dragged under the rushing river of attachment, which always flows in the opposite direction of nirvana.

Second, she rescues us from thieves. Again, there are cases where people have magically safeguarded their possessions from bandits and robbers in Tibet by praying to her. In the higher sense, she liberates us from the sneaky thief of wrong views, which steal our inner wealth of excellent qualities.

Third, she rescues us from lions. The king of the jungle looks down on all other animals, but Tara liberates us from such pride, which is the deeper meaning.

Fourth, she rescues us from snakes. Snakes slither around in the undergrowth and spread their venom to their prey, which is how jealousy operates from ignorance. So Tara liberates us from the serpent of jealousy.

Fifth, she rescues us from fire. Fanned by wrongdoing, the flames of anger destroy all our happiness and the causes of happiness. There are accounts of people being saved from house fires miraculously by Tara, and also biographies of those who have been liberated from anger by the blessings of Tara's loving-kindness. This one I find really important because fear leads to anger, and with both fear and anger, there's a strong reaction to an object perceived outside of ourselves. With anger, we behave out of control, and with fear, things feel out of our control.

Sixth, she rescues us from flesh-devouring demons. We think of demons as terrifying spirits that lurk in the shadows and bring supernatural horror. Tara liberates us from the demon of doubt, which gnaws away at our chances of accomplishing Dharma.

Seventh, she rescues us from imprisonment. Without generosity, we can't even begin to develop the transcendent perfections, so we're shackled to samsara by our avarice. Tara liberates us from the confinement of being mean and stingy.

Eighth, she rescues us from elephants. Once, a drunken wild elephant was deliberately set in the direction of Shakyamuni Buddha, though of course it couldn't kill him. The Buddha pacified him with his amazing power of love. With delusion, we're just as capable of being as wild as that, and we can lose control and trample all the good things on the path. So Tara liberates us from delusion.

These are some reflections that mean something to me and why I love Tara, but there's one more that I've found really important too. When we practice the Tara visualization in meditation—or any

Vajrayana meditation, actually—the self-generation always starts with something like "From the state of voidness . . ." Some people might think, "OK, here I am, sitting with all my faults and problems, and I try to imagine everything disappears into a state like space, then I pretend to look like this pretty lady, a much better personality than me. . . ." That's totally wrong. The profound thing is that, right from the very beginning, we stop thinking of ourselves in relative, dualistic terms. We open our hearts to the experience, the understanding of voidness, and then that mind itself manifests as Tara. It's not the ordinary "I" at all, otherwise Vajrayana practices would be counterproductive to liberation. So each time we're practicing such meditation properly, we're getting closer and closer to the realization of Tara this way. That is how we can experience the power to be really fearless, to have the fearless ultimate bodhichitta.

8
The Transformative
Power of Compassion

The Buddha of Compassion

You may already be familiar with Avalokiteshvara (or as we call him in Tibetan, Chenrezig), the bodhisattva who embodies the enlightened universal compassion of all the buddhas. For Tibetans, Avalokiteshvara is something like our patron saint. So, like all Tibetans, I felt a special connection to him from an early age. I remember first being enthralled by a painting of the four-armed Avalokiteshvara in my grandmother's room when I was sitting on her knee (I'm a bit big for that now, unfortunately!), and she told me all about Avalokiteshvara and some amazing stories. And then in Kamrao, the Indian village where I lived with my mother's family, there were also images of Avalokiteshvara, such as the form with a thousand hands that have a thousand eyes, and my Ayi (maternal grandmother) told me some stories too. But I have to admit, you know how sometimes the deities like Avalokiteshvara look almost androgynous in the traditional Tibetan paintings, since buddhas are really beyond male and female? Well, because my grandmother emphasized how Avalokiteshvara loves all sentient beings like a mother loves her only child, how those thousand eyes look out on all sentient beings, how the antelope skin he often has draped across his left shoulder symbolizes the love of a mother who would even sacrifice her own life to protect her baby, when I was a small boy I really thought of Avalokiteshvara as female, as a nurturing mother figure. Of course, that wouldn't be strange in a Chinese Buddhist family, since they usually depict Avalokiteshvara as Kwan Yin in female form.

Anyway, of course I have received countless Avalokiteshvara initiations and learned so much about "him," but I still feel a strong feminine, motherly vibration when I think of Avalokiteshvara. And so I really find the meditations and recitations of Avalokiteshvara so helpful because they help remind me of the Buddha's motherly, all-embracing love that we all need.

There are so many stories about Avalokiteshvara in Tibetan Buddhist history. We have stories about Avalokiteshvara with the very origins of Tibetan civilization and especially about some of the important early Buddhist kings such as Songtsen Gampo, who were considered emanations of Avalokiteshvara. And even today, we consider His Holiness the Dalai Lama to be the living emanation of Avalokiteshvara. I feel incredibly fortunate that I have been able to be in His Holiness's presence several times since I was born. When I was a little boy, I was just bowled over by him. When he just looked at me, I felt that the buddha of compassion was looking right at me. And as I grew up, of course I just loved him more and more. But when I first saw him reaching out to show compassion for a very simple person—not a world leader or another high-ranking monk, but an ordinary guy—caressing his cheek and wiping his tears away, I felt that was Avalokiteshvara showing me directly what the compassion he embodies is all about. I guess that's why I love His Holiness and why I love Avalokiteshvara—not that they're really any different, of course.

Why Is Avalokiteshvara So Important?

When we look at the world these days, although there are many positive developments, there is also a lot of conflict, trauma, disaster, and suffering. For instance, with conflict, it's not like in olden times when a soldier had one weapon that could strike only one other soldier at a time. We live in an age with weapons that can harm millions of people at the push of a button, and not just soldiers but so many innocent civilians too. In conflict, the thinking is very much "us" and "them," with strong attachment to "us" and then some kind of justification that gets set in the brain that it's OK to harm or have less feeling about "them." That is why we need, more than ever before, the universal compassion of Avalokiteshvara, which has no discrimination, no boundaries, no judgments or conditions.

The Lord of the Lotus Dance

Avalokiteshvara manifests in many different forms to suit the different dispositions, inclinations, and characteristics of trainees to guide us most expediently and effectively to awaken exactly the same limitless loving empathy for all sentient beings, our mothers. The particular form of Avalokiteshvara as the Lord of the Lotus Dance is a special form of Avalokiteshvara for overcoming attachment and opening up bounteous merit, which came into our Sakya tradition from the great translator Bari Lotsawa. As Bari Lotsawa said about the Lord of the Lotus Dance:

> You whose nature is beyond desire
> Yet are passionate for the passionate
> To teach in accord
> with those who are lustful and suchlike:
> To that pacifier I offer homage.

Now, the buddhas transcend all suffering, all stress, and all confusion. They have overcome the afflictive and even the subtlest cognitive obscurations that have prevented the accumulations of merit and wisdom from coming to completion. Thereby, they have awakened the truly immeasurable compassion that needs no reference of impure relative appearance. They are beyond desire, like desire to experience something better, hotter, more exciting, and more fulfilling; desire to not have to deal with the things that weary them, annoy them, upset them, or hurt them; desire to be someone else, to be somewhere else; or even desire to not have to deal with life at all, all of which, coming from being stuck in the mud of misknowing, are the sources of suffering and stress. But even though they are beyond all that, they are out of that quicksand for good, the exquisite beauty of their awakenedness means that they know exactly the right teaching for the right time and place and will always do whatever it takes to help everyone else get the hell out of the stinking pigsty that is samsara!

The Skillful Means of Transformation

As the Lord of the Lotus Dance, Avalokiteshvara, who kind of pretends to be a bodhisattva in the sutras but is really a completely perfect buddha, manifests out of his unbounded wisdom and unstoppable compassion in a passionate form that we who are on the path purifying passion can relate to in our meditation very effectively.

Due to the transcendent perfection of skillful means (*upaya* in Sanskrit), the buddhas are most capable in guiding us in this age of rampant materialism, where there's such an overload of sensory stimulation, such unchecked idealization of instant gratification, such unchecked idealization also about the way we should look, staying young forever, always keeping attention occupied by one new technological device or another, and such a seemingly endless array of choices that our modern lifestyle affords us. But will any of that really bring us true happiness? Will any of it really help accumulate merit and wisdom or really help overcome afflictive and cognitive obscurations? Really? I don't think so. So since in the Vajrayana system of Buddhist practice it is not necessary to rely only on abandoning sensory desire, but the Dharma technology is provided for us to transform desire, the particular practice of the Lord of the Lotus Dance can be a very special blessing for us in the modern age to develop more merit, wisdom, and other vital heart qualities for awakening.

The Problem with Attachment

Now, why is attachment so problematic anyway? This is something I feel we need to contemplate over and over. It's vital for us to reflect on it in reference to our felt experience rather than just as an abstract philosophical ideal.

If we look in a dictionary, I guess the opposite of attachment would be detachment. I'm a bit wary of that. The idea in Buddhism is not about becoming some kind of unfeeling robot. Any kind of trouble and strife comes up in our family or at work or at school that might disturb our so-called equanimity, and we're like, "Well, that's samsara. I'm just gonna detach. It's all just emptiness anyway. I'm off to my shrine room to do my meditation away from all this baloney because I've gotta detach!" I can't stand that kind of attitude. That's just attachment to fixed views; even if they're supposed to be Buddhist views, it's using them in the wrong way. Buddhism is about waking up, being in the moment and facing reality with wisdom and compassion, not running away into some Hogwarts of malas, bells, chants, robes, and big hats. OK, I do big hats and bells and stuff myself sometimes, because aspects of our Tibetan Buddhist culture have their place and we want to preserve them; they can be very supportive. But you know what I mean—they're not ends in themselves.

With, Not *In*

What we're really awakening to, then, is what I like to call a responsive nonattachment rather than a reactive detachment. What I mean is this: When we relate to life with wisdom and compassion, with our awareness evolved, ripened, and matured by hearing and studying the teachings, then actively contemplating those teachings, and then meditating or cultivating the teachings deep within ourselves, all upon the firm foundation of an upright, uplifting morality, then we have the awareness to be with what appears to mind, with what we're experiencing. We empower our ability to respond; we take responsibility for our lives rather than reacting and getting caught up in all kinds of stressful, painful karmic dynamics due to the entrenched habit of identification with "me" and "mine," of being stuck in the appearances to mind, which is a kind of fixating on what affects us when we forget or neglect to integrate Dharma.

I guess I use this almost as a kind of mantra: "Be *with*, not *in*, and therefore, *respond* instead of *react*." I've found it so vital and beneficial in my own life, in my own very small Dharma practice, in my understanding of what real equanimity is about.

The Way Out

We can have that primary habit, that mistaken way of being, which is the worldly way, the painful path of clinging, which can get us into a whole lot of troubl. But the good news is we have this wonderful way out, an alternative way of being: the mindful way of wisdom and compassion.

First, we need to really get a handle on what the unawakened way of clinging and attachment is all about. As the Bodhisattva Manjushri revealed to the founding father of our lineage, Sachen Kunga Nyingpo:

If there is clinging to this life,
One is not a Dharma practitioner.

If there is that primary clinging, all manner of attachments follows, as surely as night follows day. What inevitably follows that? Suffering. That is because "this life" that we experience is experienced through the senses: what we see, hear, smell, taste, touch, and mentally process. If our life is reduced to only what we experience through the six senses, then our perspective ends up being very limited.

We want to see beautiful people, beautiful places; we want to hear the kinds of sounds that make us tap our feet, lift our spirits, and validate our self-worth; we want to smell the sweetest fragrances, taste the yummiest food, and escape into thoughts of exhilarating scenarios. But seeing rotting corpses and impoverished slums? Hearing people fight or someone blame, criticize, or insult us? Smelling a foul odor? Ugh! Tasting my attempts at cooking? Always disgusting, believe me. And then thinking about what happens if one of our most respected spiritual teachers passes away, or our loved ones are in terrible pain? Unbearable, isn't it? We certainly don't want any of that, thank you very much.

All this stuff is the hazardous fuel for attachment and aversion, and as Sachen Kunga Nyingpo realized, when we cling to this life, and then the attachments to what we want and aversions to what we don't want take over, we're bound to be disappointed, to get stressed out, and to have a gnawing sense of dissatisfaction cloud over our lives.

A life without Dharma is like winning the lottery and leaving the ticket in your pocket so it ends up in the wash and gets ruined, and before you know it, the next week's numbers are drawn and it's too late. Game over. If we haven't got a handle on attachment, then how can we open the door to freedom?

One of the reasons that our teachers give teachings such as *Parting from the Four Forms of Clinging* and instructions like that again and again is not that they think we're morons and didn't get it the first time around. It's because those teachings are not introductory philosophy to get out of the way before moving on to the "real thing"—you know, the fancy higher stuff like the sophisticated tantric yogas and so on and so forth. The preliminary teachings are actually key paradigms for reflection throughout our lives. It takes honest self-appraisal and actual practice to truly feel the worth, the benefit, and the importance of these teachings. Otherwise, we can face a kind of danger, and all the higher teachings that seem fascinating because they're supposed to be "advanced" won't even work without that constant reflection first.

We make the noble effort to go to a Buddhist monastery or center to do our meditations. We recite all the right prayers to evoke immeasurable loving-kindness, compassion, empathetic gladness, and equanimity, even the most noble aspiration of bodhichitta. And as we sit there in that special place, our malas around our wrists, our bodies in the perfect meditation posture: "Oh Tara, may all sentient beings be free from suffering. . . ." Are we visualizing Mother Tara raining healing nectar on all sentient beings? Or, on the inner movie screen of our minds, do images of how we'd like to plan another awesome trip to the mall just like we did last month creep in? Or how I'm gonna look at that guy who didn't say hi back to me the other day so he thinks I don't care. How did that float in there? "Everything dissolves into voidness. . . ." Deep breath out. Ahh . . . peace. And suddenly I'm rehearsing a monologue I'm going to deliver to my neighbor, to great effect, of course, so he knows exactly how unfair and unreasonable he's been and how I'm not standing for it anymore. . . . But, of course, I'll never actually say it that way when the time comes. Yep, the mind can conjure millions of different story lines for the never-ending soap operas that get played out on our inner movie screens. And, because of how caught up our minds have been with sense stimuli, a lot of it can be just a load of garbage that surfaces for no reason too, like really annoying songs we don't even like that play over and over in our heads.

Of course, we're not blindly following the sense desires of this life all the time, otherwise we would never really be oriented to the Dharma to begin with. In *Entering the Bodhisattva's Way of Life*, Shantideva said something like:

> Those whose minds are attached to worldly possessions, due to their being in the state of distraction, have no opportunity for liberation from the suffering of samsara.

But neither are we trying to sterilize our minds so we somehow never feel any emotions. We can't just suppress what we feel, how the mind is affected by life, in the hope that we can superimpose Buddhist ideas and ideals onto our consciousness to shut out the pain and disappointment. That doesn't work either.

The stuff that arises in the mind even when we're making use of supportive conditions such as a peaceful monastery and a session of meditation practice with great teachers and fellow practitioners—we can end up in quite a quandary with what to do with it.

Sometimes, even with the best will in the world and all the strength we can muster, stuff comes up: visceral feelings, stuff that feels raw, electric, cold, right in the gut, right in the marrow and nerve plexuses of our body. When it arises, we can feel like parrots reciting our meditation texts if that stuff's not shifting. Or, perhaps worse, we could doubt the practice if we feel that it's compounding a tendency for dissociation, projecting lovely thoughts that are supposed to be compassionate and all that in theory but, when isolated to the headspace alone, are at the expense of processing what we're really feeling in the here and now.

For me, the practice has got to touch that stuff. So what has to occur for us to really feel that transformation is possible?

Wisdom without Attachment

For Dharma practitioners in general, letting go is our key. As Sakya Pandita said, we have to let go of everything we attach to. The physical renunciation that fully ordained monks and nuns commit to is all about that, isn't it? Their renunciation enables them to not just get a sense of calm occasionally; it's supposed to turbo-boost their meditation because they live by renunciation, away from the sensory distractions and proliferations that form attachment. But, of course, actual liberation is brought about from special insight, not just the peace that can come from sense restraint. Whether we practice as lay practitioners or monastic practitioners, we all need to cultivate letting go in the mind. As Sakya Pandita said, when we know the things that we get attached to as they really are, then we are truly free. And as the Buddha himself said, "Wisdom is without attachment."

Definitive Letting Go

For liberation, we must reach a level of letting go that is not only derived from committing to rules and regulations or from willpower, but a natural, uncontrived, effortless letting go.

We usually translate this as *renunciation*, but that doesn't quite work for me. I know I sometimes drive my English tutor crazy because I get so fussy about finding exactly the right words, but it's because otherwise we can end up with the wrong idea about certain aspects of Dharma practice. So *renunciation* is what's usually translated from the Tibetan *ngejung*. *Ngepa* means something certain, something definitive that we can feel, we can trust. *Jungwa* means to rise into something. It's a very positive term in Tibetan, whereas I think *renunciation* in English sounds a bit heavy—not negative, but a bit contracted maybe, like we should give up ever eating chocolate again if we want to do this properly. Miserable! So we can think of letting go in a really uplifting, positive sense, embracing what opens up in our life from dropping attachment, the stuff that gets in the way of wisdom and compassion, the stuff that compounds suffering and stress. We can trust that effortless letting go will definitely raise us into truth and freedom. That's why I translate *ngejung* as "definitive letting go," or we can even say "definitive raising up."

As Mahayana practitioners, we need to reach that effortless letting go, and this serves as a foundation for the life of our path, which is bodhichitta. Just as first we invest in joyful vigor and commit to a level of moral conduct to reach effortless letting go, so we cultivate aspiring and engaging bodhichitta and live by its course to reach effortless bodhichitta.

To reach effortlessness—effortless letting go and effortless bodhichitta—we need to first apply ourselves in the causes of the path of accumulation. For instance, we start by letting go of the gross attachments to worldly possessions by contemplating, then doing the equalizing meditations, the exchanging meditations of tonglen, and other such processes. By progressing in this way, we will enter the path of accumulation and eventually traverse the five paths, which we need to do in order to reach completely perfect bodhi, the state in which we have optimized our human potential to bring about the ultimate welfare of all wandering beings, our mothers.

For Vajrayana practitioners, we have the extraordinary means of accomplishing this. It says in the *Lankavatara Sutra* that those who see the Buddha, who is so peaceful and beyond birth and death, will purify attachment. Vajrayana practitioners obtain empowering consecration into a mandala so that we can emulate the body, speech, and mind of a buddha, not because we're imitating some kind of superior personality like an actor, but because we have been blessed by the uninterrupted stream of the Buddha's blessings through the guru, whose blessings ripen the seed of our buddha nature more expediently than any other means. This requires immense faith, in the guru and Triple Gem, of course, but also in our own potential; and immense merit too, like the merit that comes from the meditation and recitation of the Lord of the Lotus Dance.

Playing with Perception

When we work with Vajrayana meditations, there's a key tool that we're using to bring about direct realization of our tutelary deity. According to Buddhist science, when we perceive an ordinary object, there are four component factors:

1. the causal condition
2. the immediately preceding condition
3. the focal condition of what is observed, the observed object
4. the common or uncommon dominant condition

We examine this conditioning in Buddhist science for the purpose of letting go of attachment to things that form the causes for our mistaken idea of a self. So in the Vajrayana, we take the "immediate preceding condition," which is the immediately preceding moment of clarity and awareness, the mind itself, and focus all our attention and energy on the body of the tutelary deity so it serves as the causal condition for clarity and awareness of the body of the tutelary deity to arise. When we do this properly, then that visualization becomes the dominant condition and we can achieve a stable focus, a bit like when we're so captivated by an enchanting piece of music that we don't notice whatever else is going on in the room at the time.

Now, if the Lord of the Lotus Dance, for example, were an ordinary object and our mind state was ordinary, then we'd just end up with a clear perception of a made-up figure. So what? The thing is, since the Lord of the Lotus Dance is a real buddha, what we achieve is not an ordinary perception but a direct realization. And, of course, this is something extraordinary, something that heralds the dawn of Avalokiteshvara's actual wisdom and compassion manifesting in our lives. When we consider it that way, we can see how any amount of the Lord of the Lotus Dance's merit-building meditation and recitation will be of incredible benefit for oneself and everyone else on this planet we share. And we need wisdom and compassion in our world more than ever. This is what the certain result of transformation is about.

The Power of Transformation

Transformation or direct realization is not an event that takes place in some kind of isolated bubble up in the head space; it's a felt experience. The power of merit, of doing good, of recognizing how afflictive emotions such as attachment and aversion are losing their grip on our lives, gives us a field of positive energy that we can feel. So even in those moments when we feel the ripples of a difficult encounter, the residues of being dismissed or discounted, the frustration of unfulfilled fantasies, the heaviness of loneliness or not feeling heard or accepted, we have a reference with bodhichitta that is not just thought but also felt. And it's so much stronger than fear, so much stronger than anger or attachment or ignorance. And even in those moments when it feels totally overwhelming, we remember that merit, that guiding light of bodhichitta in our hearts; to have the loving-kindness and compassion for ourselves to breathe through the pain, let it go, process what's affecting Planet You and let the storm pass without judgments, without inhibitions. If we can't do that, how can we ever direct bodhichitta to any other sentient being? It has to start here.

From here, the potential for positive change is endless, because realization isn't just in the mind, it's in our lives. We become more compassionate in our hearts and then, well, just try to stop us from doing good in the world! Not just singing the mantra OM MANI PADME HUM and doing meditations, but actively helping others. Even just starting with one person, more and more, we act out of the unconditional love that is born in the mind. Building stupas and temples and all that is a source of merit, and, personally, I appreciate these things a lot, but we also need to build merit through the stuff that's not lacquered in gold: by saving animals, planting trees, stopping bullying, helping those who are impoverished. Avalokiteshvara is right there too.

Through continual cultivation of this practice, accumulating more and more merit and wisdom, we will come closer and closer to manifesting the realization and blissful compassionate qualities of Avalokiteshvara. This is why the Buddha explained that the practice of the Lord of the Lotus Dance is so powerful and expedient for attaining the qualities of Avalokiteshvara, for purifying from the mind even the subtlest latencies connected to our attachment to the three realms of samsara, and in multiplying the merit and benefits of whatever Dharma practice we do. To attain the stage of a buddha, we can't have wisdom without merit, nor can we have merit without wisdom. With the two wings of merit and wisdom together, we're ready for takeoff.

9

Victory Over All Obstacles

When I was asked to bestow an initiation for a Vajrayana practice used to dispel all the obstructive forces and corrupting influences that can affect a practitioner, I looked at the root text in the Tibetan Buddhist canon where it lists, wow, so many different entities that can cause temporal or spiritual obstacles. We've got a pantheon of weird and wonderful gods and demons that could give the ancient Greeks a run for their money. However, I'd like us to take a closer look not at a long list of invisible monsters that we've got to worry about—that's really not our goal—but at the direct sense of the disturbing obstacles signified by maras and so forth that we need to overcome in order to reach ultimate imperturbability.

Are Ghosts Real or Not?

When I first considered transmitting such a practice in the West, a dichotomy came to mind. On the one hand, in the East, belief in the paranormal is pretty much normal. The idea that there are volatile entities that might not be visible to the naked eye of ordinary people but are part of the universe we share and can cause us memory loss or weight loss or nightmares or nervous disorders and so on is not just an idea, it's a part of our cultural mentality. Conversely, in the modern Western world, this belief is far from common. In fact, most people are very skeptical about even considering such thinking, considering it to be just mythology that should be relegated to the past.

The more I considered it, the more I felt that, sure, there are dangers with any kind of fixed belief one way or another. For example, if we foster a spiritual paranoia that there are all these real and dangerous spirits out to get us and rush around feverishly collecting all these prayers and rituals that we can desperately try to use to banish them, then not only is that far from a peaceful mind to practice with, but it also ends up compromising our refuge vow, because it tends to breed the sense of relying on something other than the Triple Gem to deal with our suffering—even if it's something nominally Buddhist. Also, whether we recognize it or not, we can have a materialistic outlook that's not actually from direct insight or even from thorough logical reasoning but has been inculcated from a general belief that to be scientific is best and this must mean that anything that's unproven or can't be seen with our eyes is a load of mumbo-jumbo. "Ah, those poor primitive Asians with all their superstitious nonsense. We know that all that supernatural stuff in the sutras is just metaphorical. That makes me such a superior Buddhist who goes for the real insight and mindfulness, not all this reincarnation and karma and ghosts and goblins. In fact, why don't I just appoint myself an authority on this new and improved Buddhism, write a book about my ideas, and make a comfortable living out of it? Whoa, think of all the cool places I'll get to visit to sell my teachings. Next stop, Honolulu!"

Now, to dismiss its metaphysical aspect, reducing Buddhism to only the bits that can be molded to a merely materialistic approach, ends up contriving something other than real Buddhism. After all, the very definition of the mind we work with in Buddhism is something that is not limited to the physical sense organs and brain. That's very clear. But when the metaphysical side is blindly believed in at the cost of logical reasoning and authentic cultivation of calm abiding and special insight, then of course that can reduce the most profound wisdom the world has ever known to a fear-ridden belief system, and that's far from what the Buddha was pointing to.

Who Is Mara Then?

What did the Buddha point out? As Nagarjuna said:

> That which arises in dependence on relationships
> Is unceasing, unborn;
> Not annihilated, not permanent;
> Not coming, not going;
> Without distinction, without identity;
> The peace taught to fully pacify fabrications
> By the perfect Buddha....

Now, through misknowing this, we get caught up in the karma that creates suffering. The wheel keeps spinning as the afflictions that drive it have momentum. That is the force that makes the demon Mara manifest.

Who is Mara? Some dark-red dude with a forked tail and horns on his head? Cool in movies, but nope. Mara can manifest in many ways, but mainly there are four maras, and they certainly don't look like little demons. First is the mara of the aggregates. The aggregates are the five components of a person's psychophysical makeup: form, feeling (pleasant, unpleasant, or neutral), perception, formatives (which is basically the force of karma), and consciousness. Although they are really like an illusion, we grasp them all aggregated together as "I" and wind up in a whirlpool of suffering. In that way, we can see why the Buddha called them a mara. Second is the mara of the afflictions. Third is the mara of the lord of death. The fourth is called the mara of the son of the gods, which is like a poetic way of referring to the attraction to sense objects we so easily get lost in.

Our Inner Demons

The afflictions are like our inner demons. Whenever I confer the refuge vow on new Buddhists, more often than not I use the detailed teaching by my ancestor Chögyal Phagpa, in which he reminds us that just going for refuge is a great protection from all that is harmful. One of the reasons for this is quite evident: we are making a commitment to looking inward to reality. We're dedicating our lives to truth. By the power of realizing the truth that the real cause of our suffering and stress is not the weather, our relationships, our unfinished projects, the traffic jam making us late, the soda that's gone warm, the coffee that's gone cold, the thin-crust when we ordered deep-dish, the pimple on the end of our nose, that comment on Facebook that was way out of league—and I thought she was my friend. . . . It's the inner demons of afflictions, the disturbing emotions that are not part of the true nature of our minds but are adventitious afflictions that literally afflict us; they cause us pain, whether we recognize it at first or not. The reason my forebear gave this encouragement in relation to the basic Buddhist act of refuge is that in looking inward instead of just outward to recognize and then remove these afflictions, we are dealing with the root of our suffering. Then, if the root is treated from the inside, how can any sprouts of suffering grow?

This basic understanding is vital, because if we expect that we will be able to overcome outer obstacles by reciting mantras without working to overcome the inner root afflictions, then I have to admit, I'm very skeptical about how beneficial that could really be. But if we target our inner demons, then I'm really confident that we can become totally invincible.

The different mental events, positive and negative, that can come and go are infinite but, generally speaking, in Buddhist psychology we group them into fifty-one. Don't worry, we're not going to cover them all here—it took me months in college—but let's look at the most problematic of the annoying ones that are the roots of all the other shades of *Ouch!* and *Ugh! No thanks!*

Misknowing

The most stubborn root to deal with is misknowing. It's not really the same as ignorance, which is like, "Oh, I can't deal with his massive ego trip right now. Let's just ignore him!" In other words, you can see, but you choose to turn away. Misknowing is actually like being blind to reality. When we misknow, we mistake this ever-changing jumble of feelings and perceptions and physical form and so on to be "me." Then we think, "Hey, not another gray hair?" and "Honey, does my butt look big in this?" and "That hurt... I can't take any more" and "I just need a bit more and then everything in my life will be OK." And we're always disappointed.

All these thoughts and feelings I often describe as like the narratives on our inner movie screen. That's what we call mental consciousness. The other consciousnesses operate through the eyes, the ears, and so on. Consciousness is always oriented toward an object, external or internal. It's dualistic in that way: consciousness the subject is oriented toward the outer or inner referent or object. Some of what we see, hear, smell, taste, and touch in the outer dreamlike world we want; some we definitely don't. Some of what appears on the inner movie screen captivates our interest and makes for an entertaining arena we can escape into rather than just bear the banality of everyday existence; some keeps us awake at night, gives us a migraine, and causes contraction all the way into the solar plexus. Now, if we don't trust in our deeper awareness—the more subtle consciousness that is not conditioned by the duality of self and other, this and that, which is pure knowing; the wisdom realizing voidness in which all karmic appearances have ceased, which is the seed of a Buddha—then just processing all the emotional components of our personal narratives is not just exhausting, it's never ending.

Of course we need to pay careful attention to our emotive tones, encouraging the positive ones and processing the negative ones through discernment, and that takes us over blind spots that impede our general well-being. For instance, the body. When we practice close placement of mindfulness on the body, it's the felt sense of body in the present moment, not the visually preconceived anatomic body we see in the mind's eye. The Buddha gave us tools, like relating to the body in terms of the elements: earth, fire, water, and air; that is, the degrees of solidity, temperature, liquidity, and distension. And between all that? Space. When we meditate, we can relate to the body that way, as something much more fluid, expansive, light, electric, pliant, and flowing than a load of bones and wet, yucky junk sealed by skin and hair. That way, when we're processing even seemingly chronic tensions, the localized sore bits in our system we can associate with anxieties and unmet needs and unresolved upset and so on—where are they lodged? "Hmm, feels tight, cold, blocked . . ." but without the visual reference for it, how is it contained? "Huh, I guess around it I can feel something warm, something buzzy, something malleable." So then where does the bad stuff end and the good stuff begin? "Hey, I can feel a shift now!"

Now it's great to do this. It's really therapeutic. I sure need it. But it still involves dealing with a dualistic consciousness. Without the teachings, we wouldn't really recognize the impermanence of painful feelings, and we wouldn't recognize that this is not self. We need to practice the teachings in order to realize without any of the afflictive obscurations and also without any of the cognitive obscurations the true nature of reality, the unification of clarity and voidness.

In order to do this, we need to complete the two accumulations of merit and wisdom. In the sutras, it is explained that this takes incalculable eons—an incredibly long time. We need the determination that even if it takes that long, we're not doing this for our own welfare; we're working to reach ultimate realization because we need to reach the stage of a buddha in order to free all sentient beings, so we'll do it. However, for the bodhisattvas, who just can't bear that sentient beings will have to suffer so long and who yearn to reach full awakening as soon as possible, the Buddha taught the great secret swift path of Vajrayana. In particular, when we enter the highest level of Vajrayana practice, we will actually be able to awaken the nondual primordial wisdom of great bliss in this very lifetime–the subtlest luminescence that directly realizes voidness.

Someone who wants to achieve the awakening of bodhi first, then bring everyone else to freedom afterward, is said to have bodhichitta like a monarch, as a ruler is enthroned first and then tries to benefit their subjects afterward. Someone who wants to reach bodhi along with everyone else simultaneously is said to have bodhichitta like a ship's captain, because the ship brings everyone to their destination at the same time. Someone who wants everyone to be free first and only then will enter nirvana themselves is said to have bodhichitta like a shepherd, since a shepherd has to goad their flock into the paddock before walking through the gate. Now, a practitioner of the Vajrayana has the great compassion of the shepherd but the method of the monarch. Once we enter, if we practice with joyful vigor and keep the commitments (*samaya* in Sanskrit) and vows, we definitely can destroy misknowing at the very root.

Attachment

Until we've uprooted misknowing for good, other afflictions sprout problems for us. Sakya Pandita described them as like very hard soil. Since all our weird and wonderful thoughts and all our hopes and fears about our mistaken notion of self can be definitively let go of through the processes of meditation, Sakya Pandita encouraged us that we have the tools in meditation to crush that coarse ground of afflictions like attachment.

There are so many ways we can think about and conceive of the objective conditions that we fantasize will make the subjective identity we attach to cozy and comfortable . . . a snug little corner somewhere in samsara that won't be so bad for our fragile little ego. That basic attachment comes from misknowing reality in regard to ourselves and everything else. But as Sakya Pandita said, it's like a poisonous berry that might taste nice at first but eventually will bring us nothing but harm.

Attachment isn't just about pleasures of the senses or in relation to other people. Even advanced meditators in solitary retreat in jungles and caves can be attached to their isolation or attached to the ecstasy of their meditation, which would keep them lingering in tranquility at the expense of developing special insight. Whatever it is that we attach to, it's very simple: let go, let go, let go. Simple, but not easy. So we need to cultivate carefulness, heedfulness around all that we relate to in consciousness through the six senses. Our moral conduct supports this; our resolve supports this; but the more we practice, the more we will find that letting go gives rise to a sense of joy and lightness and clarity that empowers our nonattachment in a way that is less about willpower and more about wisdom.

Anger

Whereas the nature of attachment is to be drawn to something, to want contact with it, anger comes from being averse to something, not wanting contact with something—or, of course, someone. And it's very much tied up with fear. It's due to fear—that basic reflex that wants to shield our vulnerable sense of self—that the energy of aggression rears its ugly head. And when that energy is specifically targeted, we have anger. Anger and fear are like stronger degrees of the sense of isolation or alienation, the first being such an overwhelmingly paralyzing and devastating sensation, to me like an actual sense of cold, that our system seems to cling to the vitality, the heat, of the repelling force of aggression and anger, only to compound our suffering and enforce the sense of separation even more.

The Buddha said we have to guard against anger erupting through our three doors—body, speech, and mind. Like Shantideva says, there is no worse enemy than anger. It's so true. I don't think anyone would take interest in Buddhist teachings if they didn't recognize the truth of this – it's evident. But we still need to reflect on the variations of anger, because some of them can be a bit sneaky.

Anger disturbs our physical well-being: it induces contraction, stresses our immune system, raises our blood pressure, ruins our sleep. It even makes us ugly. Seriously! Even someone very beautiful, when they're throwing a tantrum, can go from looking like a movie star to something like a cartoon angry face drawn on a tomato or something.

Speaking from anger actually hurts. You know the saying "Sticks and stones may break my bones but words will never hurt me?" Tibetans have something similar. Well, sorry, I don't agree with that at all. I'm with the Buddha on this one. Words can be weapons of mass destruction! I can put on a brave face and say, "Just ignore that" until I'm blue in the face, but when someone says something really hurtful, it can feel like a red-hot poker going right into my solar plexus. I think we have to be very careful with things like this because there's sometimes a danger that in referring to the ultimate goals of Buddhism that the aryans realize, and also in encouraging the virtues of their patience and so on, we can trivialize a suffering that actually requires immediate, not eventual, action. Educating ourselves and one another in what bullying is—I feel very passionate about that. I say it that way because intention is the key, and sometimes, due to ignorance, we may not mean it, we may not realize it, but our words are hurting someone. Personally, I don't want to do that to anyone if I can help it. Especially in a culturally diverse country, we have to learn from talking to people, taking an interest in their culture, their community identity, without any biases. We can't just stick our noses up in the air and say, "Everything in samsara is illusory. Get over yourself!" Let's make sure we don't forget that on the receiving end, being sensitive is not the same as being *affected*. Our practice of developing wisdom and compassion actually makes us more sensitive—fully sensitive. But, at the same time, we develop inner strength, patience, and insight from this practice, so, according to our own capacity, we will find that we can be less and less affected—stressed, rattled, disheartened—by mistakes made by others who still have to work through their stuff.

One year on my birthday, a particular monk who unfortunately seemed rather unhappy most of the time—I don't know why—came up to me abruptly and said with a miserable face, "Another year closer to death for ya!" Um, yeah, about that: When a great master like Dilgo Khyentse Rinpoche would say that with a big warm smile, it was a lovely playful reminder of a key Buddhist teaching. The important thing is not what's officially Buddhist or even true, it's our intention and empathy for others. I didn't lose sleep over that interaction, but it did make me think about the importance of our intentionality in relation to speech.

So we need to check our intention and check the anger in our mind. Here there's something serious to consider. Some people think that we actually need anger to deal with problems in the world. For example, if we look at some of the social injustices, the horrors going on in the world or even in our own communities, we can feel outrage and become enraged about it. The crucial thing here is the difference between reacting and responding. It is not cool to dismiss the suffering in the world because it threatens our fragile conditioned idea of personal peace. A bodhisattva needs to feel an irrepressible urge to do something to help the world, but that is the strength of great compassion, not anger. Anger is an affliction that, by its very nature, defiles the clarity of our mind streams and impedes our ability to use the full capacity of our human intelligence. That's not the state we want to be in to help others fully. In the short term, maybe the adrenaline of anger can give us a drive to fight for a cause, but long term? Phew, exhausting! Compassion, on the other hand, only serves to enrich our minds and sustain our determination. Then even if we have to deal with something that requires a forceful expression, it's an informed response rather than a reaction that leaves a funny taste in the mouth.

For example, I love my cousin's young children with every fiber of my being. I couldn't get angry with them even if I tried. But if I saw one of them reaching for something on a counter that had a kettle or something on it that could injure them, you better believe I would scream at the top of my lungs for them to stop. Maybe they'd be upset at first, because they wouldn't realize without seeing the kettle why I was shouting, but afterward they'd quickly feel OK with lots of big hugs, and I wouldn't feel any regret.

Then there's another thing with anger that those of us born into Buddhist and probably other religious cultures will be familiar with. Once, a monk came to see me about something on his mind. He was visibly upset, even scared. He said, "Rinpoche, I feel I can trust you. I need your advice. I want to tell you something I've never told anybody." And it took him some time to muster the courage, and finally he said, "Rinpoche, sometimes I get angry." I was like, "Uh-huh, OK, yeah, then...? Wait, what, that's it?!" It turned out he wasn't angry at anyone or anything in particular, but he had this festering rage that would come up and make him so frustrated. Um, welcome to the club! This is because a cultural disdain for expressing anger isn't the same as a personal commitment to implementing the practices to transform and overcome anger. In fact, we can't respond instead of react if we don't first face fear and aggression when it arises in our system, honestly and unconstrained. Otherwise, we'll just be repressed, which is not healthy. Facing it, feeling it, but then letting go and trusting in the heart's original purity. We don't have to "accept" anger, exactly, as a sign of something that masks deeper psychological issues—that's never ending and tends to take us into narratives rather than the present-moment reality—but be open to everything and anything that appears in the mind from that basic sense of dualistic separation. And then let it go. This uncovers something much more important: clarity and wisdom.

Pride

With the dualistic sense of separation that comes from misknowing, like when we don't understand dependent origination, we get stuck in a consciousness that is afflicted. In that desert, certain buzzards follow in attendance, namely, the basic delusion about a self, a fixed self-view, taking pride in that self, and clinging to it. This are the process with which delusion about a self takes hold. And the whole process comes undone in blissful wakefulness when wisdom is developed.

So of course, in shielding the so-called self, deciding who we are, what we are, and all that jazz, pride can afflict the mind.

Sometimes pride means thinking we're better than others. It might not be shown openly, but it can be harbored under the surface, like Uriah Heep for those of you who, like me, enjoy reading Charles Dickens's books—"Oh, I'm ever so humble!"

The more evident form of pride we call "more proud than proud"—in other words, being a show-off. Worse is inverted pride, being proud of bad habits and deeds, like, "Yeah, I'm the best bully ever. Everyone's scared of me, and I'm so good at humiliating people!" Um, really?

Then it can be subtler than those, like a novice in the company of very senior monks who are very learned and experienced, but thinking, "Well, I'm nearly as good as them." Not yet, junior; back to your studies! Or one might not be proud in general but have pride about certain qualities that aren't really there, like someone who thinks after a comparatively small amount of practice, "Wow, I've been to meditation classes six weeks in a row. Now I'm an adept meditator." Steady there....

And then it gets even subtler. We might be genuinely humble, a really sensible person, but from the Buddhist point of view, just thinking "I am" is actually a form of pride. So with this and any other form of pride, we need the skill of our own self-awareness and the applied wisdom that understands that no matter how much we've fallen into the trap of pride, pride is the prop to the delusion of self but it's not self. And we need to remember this in regard to others because it's all too easy to point out, "Hey, look at this guy. He's so stuck up! Thinks he's so much better than anyone else. I can't deal with that." Perceiving faults in others, pride or whatever it may be, almost inevitably becomes a form of pride in itself. That's why, relatively speaking, we need to focus on appraising our own faults with wisdom, without beating ourselves up, and only look at the qualities in other people. Then, ultimately, the wisdom realizing the voidness of self and all phenomena will remedy every aspect of conceit for good.

Doubt

Reflecting on these inner demons like this isn't disheartening but an encouragement that the fruits of Dharma practice will bring us victory over the obstacles from afflictions. What will dishearten us or make us waver in this is doubt, the afflicted awareness that's uncertain because it's always stuck in a tug-of-war between two possibilities: "Am I really wasting my time with this? Am I still an emotional wreck? Why am I still getting angry and scared? Maybe it's because my obstacles are just too big? Maybe I should be doing a different kind of meditation?" And on and on like that.

For me, I have to admit, growing up with a lot of faith in Buddhism meant that I didn't have much doubt—or so I thought. Sometimes doubts can lie dormant when we have only a superficial rather than informed faith in Dharma. When I was really young, I think I perceived the Buddha as God. Then I started to think like someone doubting their god might think: "If he can save all sentient beings, why hasn't he already?" When, after learning properly and thinking about it, and I got it—that the Buddha helps us by showing us the path but that we have to actually do the practice—I was relieved, because the idea that the Buddha was a powerful god who wasn't doing his job properly just didn't sit well with me at all. So the key to unlocking the door of doubts is, provisionally, developing faith through reasoning and, ultimately, through seeing truth directly.

Although it is up to each of us to do the practice, to see the truth for ourselves to overcome uncertainty, the irony is that a healthy level of skepticism is needed. But skepticism isn't the same as cynicism. We need a sharp intellect that can question the assumptions of the relative mind and remain objective. We really get to exercise that in a Tibetan monastery's dialectics program. Cynicism would be more that we continually try to find faults in the sound counsel of our teachers and so on, and we lose our objectivity and context.

Views

We lose our objectivity when we have fixed views, views about self, others, the world, the meaning of life, and whatever else that is anywhere from perversely wrong to falling short of direct perception. In his *Root Stanzas on the Middle Way Entitled "Wisdom"* Nagarjuna praised the Buddha because, caring dearly out of a loving heart, he taught the holy Dharma for the abandoning of all views. Considering that views prevent direct perception of the holy Dharma from being uncovered, they are afflictions too.

Viewing the five aggregates, which are conditioned and in constant flux, as the seat for an intangible soul is an affliction. In the Sakya philosophical tradition, it is very important to recognize views that are one of the four limiting extremes: what is eternalistic, nihilistic, positing phenomena as neither existent nor nonexistent, or positing them as both. Wrong views such as "That race is more evolved than that one" or "Men are better at that than women" or "They shouldn't have the same rights as us normal people" or "Ah, there's no such thing as karma and the Buddha wasn't really enlightened"–those are *major* afflictions. Viewing our views as higher than or equivalent to liberating wisdom—wrong! Viewing religious codes and rites, as supportive as we might think they are on the relative level, as the actual way to liberation—wrong again!

And be warned, trying to have no views is a view too. Freeing ourselves from really wrong views through learning, reasoning, and so on is the primary foundation, and then, in filtering the mind of subtler misperceptions, the Madhyamaka or Middle Way approach we favor in Tibetan monasteries is not so much about establishing a view but about challenging the consequences of our unchecked assumptions about reality. Kunkhyen Gorampa said:

> Whatever is experienced is one's own mind.
> That very mind, a mere collection
> Of causes and conditions, is illusory.
> Knowing illusion without any fabrications,
> One meditates on ultimate reality.

Peace and Happiness

Gradually, through developing this insight, we will be able to conquer all our demons inside and out. What's important is that we maintain the determination that we will do this and we will do it in order to benefit all mother sentient beings.

When we have that determination, that aspiration, then the peace this brings is not passive. It is the blossoming of our buddha nature, like the sun emerging from behind the clouds. The pacification of obstacles and negativity when we have that aspiration will naturally awaken the dynamic expression of the bodhisattva's nonviolent, altruistic, peaceful mind.

Ordinary happiness comes and goes, sure, but the ultimate happiness that arises from the blossoming of our buddha nature is beyond fluctuating conditions, beyond all karma.

The nature of a buddha is to directly help, to benefit in every way possible, for the short term and long term, all sentient beings—to bring everyone to the ultimate peace and happiness.

10
Questions for the Modern Practitioner

Is happiness just more attachment?

No, not *just* more attachment. The Buddha did point out that our wanting, our desires, cause suffering. But also, we have to want to attain the liberation or enlightenment in order to start practicing Buddhism. These two things are not contradictory, in fact. So once we attain the goal of liberation or enlightenment, then all karma ceases, which means we have gone beyond wanting; there's nothing more to want when we reach that goal. In the meantime, when we're still on the path, we have to refrain from the unvirtuous karma that will compound our own and others' sufferings, and we have to practice meditation and so on to reach the goal. Now, from the point of view of impure vision, the ordinary worldly point of view, we get happiness from sensory experiences, like seeing beautiful things, listening to beautiful sounds, tasting beautiful foods, and so on.

In Buddhism we also talk about the mind as the sixth sense, so this includes the pleasant memories of the past we like to think about, and the ideas and ambitions for the future we like to create, as well as the fantasies that we create to try to make another version of now in samsara different from the now that we're really experiencing. This is never really satisfying. So in Buddhism, when we recognize that all those things that stimulate the mind—from the outside through the senses, and through the jumble of our thoughts and emotions—are not reliable or permanent, we don't plunge into depression or try to become like an unfeeling robot. Instead, we develop a more stable and reliable sense of contentment in the mind that is not dependent on other things. This state is actually much freer and more blissful than what we can find from the outside. Then, generally speaking, we can enjoy sensory things without attachment so long as they are not unvirtuous. So Buddhism can bring us more happiness, a deeper happiness, not just on the ultimate level but in ordinary terms too.

How can we deal with everyday stress?

First of all, whether we are still studying, or we are already working in whatever our chosen field is, or we are busy raising a family and so on, it's really important that we take time each and every day, even if it's just a bit, to practice some meditation. Even just a few minutes will be of immense benefit. You can do some calm-abiding meditation by visualizing the Buddha or attuning to the in-and-out breathing and do some prayers that fill you with inspiration and remind you of the stages of the path. Otherwise, even if we really love the idea that practicing Buddhism can help us to be calmer, kinder, more insightful, and so on, it won't really come to life unless we feel it deep inside from meditating. So even if your workload feels enormous, *make* time to meditate, and it will help. Not only can it make you feel less stressed, it will also make your mind sharper and clearer for your studies, your work, or whatever. Then, to do it effectively, we must be mindful of the present, not caught up in ideas about the future or the past, so we have to let go of all those ideas when we meditate. The more we do it, the more we feel clarity and confidence about what to do with our lives that will be beneficial.

So be kind to yourself, don't give up studying hard and working hard, because those are good things to do, but familiarize yourself with a daily practice and you will really start to notice changes.

How do we deal with distraction and lack of support from non-Buddhist friends?

First, I think there are more and more serious Buddhist practitioners and centers where you can learn Buddhist philosophy and join in the meditation, so although you don't have to completely abandon your old friends, you can try to spend more time in the centers where you will meet like-minded people who will support you in your practice. If those things are hard to find, then you need to have self-reliance. Make a determination to yourself to spend so much time each day or each week studying and practicing. Then even if your friends hassle you and say, "Hey, don't be so boring! Why not come out with us now?" or something like that, you will have the self-discipline to politely decline; then later, if you're free, of course you can spend time with your friends if you want to, but you won't feel pressured or like you're forced to go along with the crowd.

I think that we shouldn't preach ideas, even good ideas about Buddhism and so on, to our friends, but rather try to be an example. What I mean is that we shouldn't get caught up in bad behavior or doing unskillful things, like drugs and so on, due to peer pressure. But we can try to show our friends that the Dharma has brought us more calm, more peace, more understanding, and so on; then, in that way, guiding them away from unskillful activities to a skillful way of life, we can show that we are a true friend. Whether they want to listen or not is up to them, of course. But I tend to find that if we preach too much, then people–young people especially, and I know because I still am one–can feel as if they're not really being listened to, as if they're always judged or disappointing, and then more lonely. So without getting caught up in distractions or unskillful things, have patience, have discipline, have love, and just listen without judgment to your friends, and you can nurture your own practice as well as inspire others to find the Dharma.

Since Mahayana Buddhism is all about love for our fellow man, is it better to be in a relationship rather than be a monk or nun?

First, I have to say it's not about love for our fellow human; it's about love for women, men and all sentient beings! Then, sure, if you are in a relationship, you can still practice Mahayana Buddhism. But being in a relationship in the romantic sense or the family sense isn't really the way to learn the love that the Buddha talked about in the Mahayana teachings. Loving someone close to you is easy because it comes naturally. In a relationship, even if you love another person, still sometimes there can be disagreements or obstacles, so we have to have strong love and other qualities such as patience and morality to overcome those obstacles. But the unconditional love of a bodhisattva has to extend to all sentient beings near and far, no matter what. Romantic love can even bring us more obstacles, as it tends to bring more attachment. So whether lay person or monk or nun, the important thing is to practice as much as we can every day to have more love and compassion for all sentient beings, no matter what the circumstances, because then we will have bodhichitta, and that is what we are aiming for in Mahayana Buddhism.

How long can we practice Buddhism before the world ends? Are there any prophecies about the world ending due to environmental disasters such as climate change?

Well, we have this moment. Although I take a lot of interest in ecological matters, in terms of practice, I personally don't worry too much about the future, because the time to practice is always *right now*— this present moment. That's really important. But yes, there are statements in Buddhism about how everything, including our own planet, which we take for granted, is impermanent, but there is no way to know exactly when this world will end. So I think more important than prophecies or anything like that is to recognize that we want our planet to be a secure inheritance for our children and grandchildren, so we have to do more to take care of our environment, the endangered species, and so on. In fact, from the Buddhist point of view, it's not just for our children and grandchildren but also for ourselves, if we want a favorable human rebirth to reconnect with the Dharma. So, for example, to take care of the environment, we each have our part to play, like ensuring we recycle, and if there isn't a local recycling scheme, then as a community we can ask our community leaders to implement one. We can teach the importance of ecological responsibility in our schools. We can adopt a vegetarian diet or, if that is not possible, a diet with a reduced meat intake. Everyone can contribute something. And in terms of our way of thinking, we can do prayers and meditations so that we are all really motivated to live a more ecologically sound lifestyle. Personally, when I first learned about global warming, I was so shocked and very concerned about the future of Mother Earth; I couldn't believe the extent of the damage done by human greed. But now, although of course I think it's still very serious, I feel more optimistic because so many people, especially young people, are motivated and doing things to help. I hope that movement keeps growing stronger and stronger.

What is the best way to meditate?

As I mentioned briefly, the stages of calm-abiding meditation are best to learn from a proper teacher rather than from books. Having said that, there is a text that all traditions of Tibetan Buddhism cherish, which is very good for giving an idea of how to meditate: *The Stages of Meditation*, by the ancient Indian scholar Kamalashila. I think there are translations easily available nowadays in English as well as commentaries by contemporary masters such as His Holiness the Dalai Lama. The foundation is that you learn about karma and morality, feel faith and devotion to the guru and Triple Gem, and gather merit. Once you're familiar with the preliminaries, learn the best posture to support a calm mind, which we call the seven-point posture of Vairochana. Then you can learn objective meditation, like visualizing the Buddha or attuning to your breath energy and so on; or subjective meditation, like cultivating loving-kindness; whichever is best for you to calm down the erratic flow of thoughts, all the internal images and sounds, and bring you to a state of single-pointedness that is very light, blissful, and concentrated. With regular practice, which means we need joyful vigor and enthusiastic commitment, we will definitely experience samadhi.

As Buddhists, what charitable causes should we support?

I think any worthy cause is good, especially those that help the poor, the sick, and the elderly, as well as the environment, endangered species, and also antibullying, conflict resolution programs, and so on. These are all very worthy causes to support. There are so many. We can't help all of them, but whatever we are able to do with the right motivation will be very beneficial. In Buddhism, offerings are often made to the monastic community who do special Buddhist practices, study full time, do retreats, keep the vows of the Buddha, teach the Dharma, and so on, so that Buddhism as a living lineage remains in our world, which is why it's called the greatest field of merit. This gives it some special relevance for Buddhists, but we also try to be charitable and kind to all sorts of good causes if we can.

How can we make a real difference in the world?

In whatever we can do right now, even if it seems quite a modest amount, if we apply ourselves with joyful vigor to what is positive and virtuous, and if we determine with insight and commitment to avoid what is negative and unvirtuous, then little by little we are planting the seeds of positive change to arise in ourselves, in our families, in our communities, in our country, and in this planet we call Earth—our home.

Think about what you can do to make a difference, whatever that might be. Don't feel discouraged or pessimistic, even in the face of adversity. Feel a sense of unity, trust, hope, and confidence in yourself and in others, just as His Holiness the Dalai Lama has encouraged us to and has exemplified in his amazing activities for so long.

In the Jataka stories and other sacred texts, we have numerous examples of how the bodhisattva who later manifested enlightenment as Shakyamuni Buddha cultivated the transcendent perfections of patience and so forth over countless lifetimes. He never gave up hope in himself or in his mission, but out of compassion, he worked tirelessly all by himself to complete the accumulations of merit and wisdom. Now, due to amazing virtues that we have accumulated in previous lives, we have the amazing good fortune to meet with the teachings of the Buddha, with the authentic teachers, and with the Sangha in harmony. Not only that, but we are not alone in this life of Dharma. So we should reflect on that good fortune and resolve to do whatever we can to not waste this precious life in Dharma but to enable the precious jewel of the Dharma to keep shining brighter and brighter.

11

Being a Twenty-First-Century Buddhist

One day at New Year's I thought, "Hmm. What's the most important thing we all, including myself, should reflect on at this time?" And I found myself forming phrases like "Be a good person; have a warm heart; don't hurt anyone; try to keep the Dharma flourishing...." Uh-huh, yep; that all sounds fine, I thought, but something just didn't feel quite right. I reflected on how that really felt to me and had to admit that we have heard that kind of thing a lot. What really will inspire change in our hearts? What will really wake *me* up?

For this, I think we need to take a closer look at the advice of His Holiness the Dalai Lama when he says we need to be twenty-first-century Buddhists. That doesn't mean we need to use iPads instead of paper scriptures. It means that we need to really analyze, to investigate deeply, what the meaning of Buddhist spirituality and science is, rather than having a superficial relationship with the Dharma.

For example, I learned one thing not from a sacred text or formal teaching but from a ten-year-old girl. When I was a small boy, playing outside with other boys, one of my female cousins came to join in when we were messing around, which didn't seem right to me at the time–I've no idea why–and I told her she shouldn't. She was upset and asked me why. I gave an answer that was the worst thing I could have said and haunts me to this day. My mind went blank as I didn't really know why, but I said, "Because you're a girl." Of course, I thought being male meant being higher than a girl, that we could do things girls cannot. I kept asking myself, "Why did I say that? Why do I think that? Is that what I really feel? Does it even make sense?" Because it doesn't make sense; it's nonsense! Now, that might seem like nothing important to some people, but it sticks in my mind because, actually, it is entirely contradictory to the teachings of the Buddha, who emphasized so often and so eloquently that we are all the same, whether male or female, rich or poor, and so on. For those guys who think, "Well, yes, BUT . . ." this is just a fact, so deal with it.

Like with the little story from my childhood, we talk about how we're all the same, love all sentient beings as if they're our mothers, and so on and so forth, but we need to make sure that this is more than just words and that we live by these teachings, right? We need to at least be aware of the differences between real Dharma and conduct that's in accord with Dharma on the one hand, and cultural norms, values, and customs on the other. Otherwise there is the danger of falling into "Lamaism," as the Western scholars who first made contact with Tibetans in the nineteenth century called it–a term I know His Holiness the Dalai Lama can't stand!

I don't believe that the richness of Buddhist culture is sustained or thrives by our lacquering gold onto statues, building stupas like skyscrapers, fussing about the hierarchical order in which lamas sit on their thrones, insisting on stuffy social formalities all the time, or dismissing scientific concerns about global warming as "nothing to do with us."

Some have called Buddhism a "science of mind" rather than a religion, and Tibetan Buddhism encompasses such a rich spirituality and philosophy that, rather than being undermined by scientific findings and advances, it is actually very compatible with and even enhanced by science. Now I'm not calling for all of us to become professors with white coats in a laboratory, but what I think we need to do is become *like* scientists when it comes to our Buddhist culture.

For instance, His Holiness the Dalai Lama was the first recipient of the Nobel Peace Prize who was awarded the prize in part because of what a pioneer of environmentalism he has been. What a disgrace it would be if we as followers of His Holiness don't play our part in saving the planet? We can't be in the background with such things; we need to stand tall working for a better world.

Once, at a place I stayed in India, the students had a few days' vacation after a long semester of studies, and afterward, I couldn't help but notice a lot of garbage around the grounds where they had been relaxing and playing games. I didn't want to just scold the students, but I offered a seminar where I explained the link between science and Dharma in dealing with ecological issues. After that, the students said they would be more diligent about avoiding waste and in recycling, in caring for animals and the environment, and for promoting education about these crucial matters. This encouraged me that education is the key.

His Holiness the Dalai Lama says, "Try to help others, and if you can't do that, at least try not to hurt them." If we want to take this advice, we should try to not simply nod in agreement and sit on our cushions praying for the environment or for social concerns. We must be pioneers. We've got to get up off our cushions and take the Dharma out into the world, applying and integrating bodhichitta into our everyday lives. In other words, now more than ever, we've got to walk the talk.

Now, I'm not saying that I'm an expert in these things, and I'm talking to myself more than anyone else. But I remember that when I first learned about global warming and the threats that many endangered species and many countries face, I was so shocked, I felt quite powerless. When I learned that the Tibetan plateau and many of the rare species there face particular ecological dangers, I felt even sadder. When I learned that so much of northern India and other parts of South Asia are dependent on Tibet for water and so these dangers can affect many millions of people and creatures, well, my mind just froze. However, when I found out that so many overseas friends wanted to do something to help and that there was more education these days about energy alternatives to fossil fuels, about recycling schemes, about protecting special habitats and animals, and so on, then I felt more optimistic. Because no one can do this alone.

We have to work together. Together, a brighter future is possible. Together in Dharma, the brightest future possible is possible too.

Identity

What does it mean to be committed to Dharma in our lives? I'm not talking about studying texts or performing rituals in monastic institutions; I'm talking about our own individual spiritual development. And in the particular context of Tibetan Buddhism, we must remember that there is no so-called spiritual life separate from our everyday life. Our spirituality has to infuse the very fabric of our precious human existence, whoever we are, wherever we live, whatever we do.

So whether we are studying a profound text, or practicing a sophisticated meditation system, or even if we only know the mantra OM MANI PADME HUM and try to have a good heart, what's it all for? What are the real benefits? How will all these things help our lives and the world we share? Here, we need a twofold approach: on the one hand, there is the internal aspect of mental, emotional, and spiritual maturation; on the other hand, how is this applied externally? If someone's turning a prayer wheel all day long with one hand but violently slapping their children into obedience with the other instead of trying methods of empathetic communication; if someone recites OM MANI PADME HUM with one corner of their lips but knocks back excessive liquor with the other side, there's a contradiction, isn't there?

The important thing is, what's actually the essence of Dharma? To be a good human being, a responsible, kind human being. But what does that mean? Some might think that Buddhists want to attain this so-called enlightenment, away from all worldly concerns. So all this stuff about human rights, equality, ecology, and so forth. "Yeah, right, whatever. I'm sure that's all well and good, but I just need to get my empowerments from my teacher tucked away in his temple, and then practice for my enlightenment so eventually, sometime in the distant future, I can be of use to sentient beings; but in the meantime, all that other stuff is irrelevant; that's nothing to do with it." Really? If enlightenment is separate from human rights, equality, freedom, then I don't want it. Sorry, but that's a fact.

At the other end of the spectrum, the culture of rampant materialism is based on the foundation of self-concern. Its main goal is to fuel our desires for instant gratification with no regard for the truth of dependent arising or the toll it takes on our inner development or our environment. If we don't see through that conditioning, we are in danger of using Dharma as a mere adjunct to our lives in order to deal with stress and losing sight of the much greater potential that the Dharma has to transform our minds and empower our communities. But actualizing that amazing potential is not just a matter of immersing ourselves in all the culture and customs that Buddhism has adapted to in Asia; it's about awakening something within ourselves that can be of benefit to everyone. That has to be our focus if we want to offer the world something more than what materialism has to offer.

The reason I want to emphasize the core values and deeper meaning of Buddhist culture as what we really need to take to heart is that putting them into practice in the modern age involves an awkward balancing act that some of us may feel we are working out in our minds. At one extreme, some people have tried encouraging me to focus on outer signs of glory and prestige as a way to show off our culture or our particular lineage. Yeah, tried, but failed miserably, I might add. At the other extreme, some people say, "Oh yeah, Buddhism is in the West now, so we don't need all these rituals and stuff. Let's just do away with all these tired old traditions and just be modern Buddhists." Whatever *that* is. In taking the core values and deeper meaning of Dharma to heart, I hope we don't need to feel that we're working a juggling act like this. I hope we can stop trying to wear a mask or dig ourselves into a rabbit hole of an inadaptable institution; that we can be authentic in our approach. In other words, let's keep it real.

For instance, we have found that rather than being an opposing force to Buddhism, science is in fact compatible and complementary to it. So, as His Holiness the Dalai Lama has pointed out, just as the Indian Buddhist masters of ancient times, especially from Nalanda University, composed their classic Buddhist texts to cover many different Buddhist and non-Buddhist perspectives, we need to learn how Buddhism is relevant to a wider society. The later texts composed by Tibetan scholars, as wonderful as they are, mainly address a purely Buddhist audience. But if we bear in mind that they were building on the foundation of the tradition of Nalanda University, we can see that learning across a broader field of modern studies is not only OK, but is also vital for enabling our own tradition to be of value to the world, especially for members of the younger generation, such as myself. We can take that broader understanding and respect of different views and approaches, and then show how Tibetan Buddhism is vast and profound in what it presents for spiritual and social progress.

I feel that the richness of Tibetan Buddhism has so much to offer the world, not through converting people to follow it as a religion, because not everyone will find it the spiritual tradition for them, but through what we as practitioners—those of us who are born into it as Tibetans and those from other cultures who adopt it because of the resonance that it has for them—can do from really practicing its core values and teachings as members of human society.

In the last century, there was a danger that this precious jewel would be lost forever, but due to the work of so many courageous and indefatigable Tibetan women and men, we are so fortunate that it is still here for us to utilize in freedom. Now that we have this incredible opportunity, we must make sure that this jewel does not become just an exotic cultural relic archived in the annals of history, but remains a thriving force for wisdom and compassion, peace and positive change to flourish on our planet for the benefit of all sentient beings. This is my heartfelt wish. And if it strikes a chord with you, I hope you will join me in doing the best thing possible in return, by trying to put it into practice.

ABOUT THE AUTHOR

Avikrita Vajra Rinpoche was born in Seattle, Washington, in 1993 into the Khon family—a Tibetan family whose ancestry can be traced back to the earliest origins of Buddhism in Tibet over a thousand years ago. The Khon family's ancestral homeland is the town of Sakya in Central Tibet, and the town's name gave rise to the Sakya Buddhist tradition, whose history is inextricably intertwined with that of the Khon family. Every generation of the Khon family has produced exemplary Buddhist scholars, practitioners, and teachers, and although the Sakya tradition has a somewhat low profile in the West, it is respected by other Tibetan traditions for its standards of scholarship and the integrity of its meditation practice.

Avikrita Vajra Rinpoche is a leading figure in the latest generation of Sakya scholars, practitioners, and teachers. He received a formal Buddhist education from the age of four when he relocated to Dehra Dun in northern India and studied under many of the key teachers of his lineage including His Holiness the Sakya Trichen and His Holiness Jigdal Dagchen Rinpoche. Beyond his academic education, he has completed many extensive meditation retreats. He began giving Dharma teachings in 2012 to both Tibetans and Westerners, and shortly after that to Chinese Buddhists in countries such as Hong Kong. His English teachings combine a readily accessible style with clear knowledge and understanding of the Dharma.

These days Avikrita Vajra Rinpoche spends much of the year at the Dzongsar Institute in Himachal Pradesh in India, where he continues to study, teach, and undergo retreats. When not at the Dzongsar Institute, he travels extensively to the USA, UK, Europe, Nepal, Taiwan, Hong Kong, and many other countries to give teachings and initiations. He also encourages people to put down their books and get up from their meditation cushions from time to time and put Buddhist teachings into action by helping others through his Marici Fellowship, which coordinates local community welfare projects. He also established the Bhadracarya Foundation in Nepal to maintain annual Buddhist activities in Lumbini, the birthplace of the Buddha, and he heads the Sakya Monastery of Tibetan Buddhism in Seattle as well as the Sakya Heritage Society in New Delhi.